# An Invitation from the Publisher

People who buy this guide have two things in common. They disdain the slick and the tacky, when it comes to lodgings. And they insist upon character and quality. You are evidently one such person, and we welcome you to the guide. You will benefit from the direct experience of thousands like yourself, travelers who spurned the Hiltons and the Holiday Inns, sought out delightful places to stay—and then were kind enough to write and tell us about them.

Will you in turn, as you travel, consider yourself an active member of this informal, beneficent fellowship and contribute your judgments to the existing treasury? Your letters to the guide, candidly reporting on hotels and inns that meet your standards—both those included here and new ones you may find—will greatly assist other travelers. They will also encourage those splendid people across the land, the new breed of hoteliers and innkeepers, who are rapidly giving America a reputation for superb hospitality.

In the back of the guide you will find forms on which you can make your reports. Use them, or compose as you will. The important thing is to write. To be vital, the guide needs fresh reports each year on every inn—to note the ones that have slipped and to affirm that the others are still wonderful.

We look forward to hearing from you.

Thomas Congdon
Publisher

# States and Canadian Provinces Covered in This Edition

UNITED STATES

Alaska
Arizona
Arkansas
California
Colorado
Hawaii
Idaho
Iowa
Kansas
Louisiana
Minnesota
Missouri
Montana
Nebraska

Nevada
New Mexico
North Dakota
Oklahoma
Oregon
South Dakota
Texas
Utah
Washington
Wyoming


CANADA

British Columbia
Ontario


# Also in This Series

*America's Wonderful Little Hotels and Inns, Eastern Region* (edited by Barbara Crossette)

*Europe's Wonderful Little Hotels and Inns* (edited by Hilary Rubinstein)

# America's Wonderful Little Hotels and Inns

## Western Region

**Fourth Edition**

Edited
by
Barbara
Crossette

*Drawings by*
*Ron Couture*
*Assistant Editor*
*Jan L. Shannon*

Congdon & Weed, Inc.
New York

Copyright © 1984 by Barbara Crossette
and Hilary Rubinstein Books Ltd.
Illustrations copyright © by Ron Couture

Library of Congress Cataloging in Publication Data

Main entry under title:

America's wonderful little hotels and inns, western region.

Previous eds., covering both eastern and western regions, published as:
America's wonderful little hotels and inns.
Includes indexes.
1. Hotels, taverns, etc.—West (U.S.)—Directories.
2. Hotels, taverns, etc.—Canada, Western—Directories.
I. Crossette, Barbara. II. Shannon, Jan L.
III. America's wonderful little hotels and inns.
TX907.A618    1984b      647′.94701        83-23992
ISBN   0-86553-111-0 (pbk.)
ISBN   0-312-92022-9 (St. Martin's Press: pbk.)

Published by Congdon & Weed, Inc.
298 Fifth Avenue, New York, N.Y. 10001
Distributed by St. Martin's Press
175 Fifth Avenue, New York, N.Y. 10010
Published simultaneously in Canada by Methuen Publications
2330 Midland Avenue, Agincourt, Ontario M1S 1P7

Cover design by Krystyna Skalski
Cover illustration by Steven Guarnaccia
Maps by Donald Pitcher

All Rights Reserved
Printed in the United States of America
Second Printing

# Contents

*Preface*     *vii*

**Part One:  Far West and Hawaii**     1

*Arizona*     *3*
*California*     *10*
*Hawaii*     *61*
*Nevada*     *65*
*Utah*     *67*

**Part Two:  Plains, Northwest, and Alaska**     71

*Alaska*     *73*
*Idaho*     *75*
*Montana*     *77*
*North Dakota*     *80*
*Oregon*     *82*
*South Dakota*     *93*
*Washington*     *95*
*Wyoming*     *106*

# Part Three:   Southwest and South Central   111

*Arkansas*           *113*
*Colorado*           *117*
*Kansas*             *131*
*New Mexico*         *133*
*Oklahoma*           *140*
*Texas*              *142*

# Part Four:   Midwest   153

*Iowa*               *155*
*Minnesota*          *158*
*Missouri*           *165*
*Nebraska*           *168*

# Part Five:   South   171

*Louisiana*          *173*

# Part Six:   Canada   179

*British Columbia*   *181*
*Ontario*            *185*

# Maps                193

# Hotel Reports       201

# Index by State      205

# Index by Inn Name   211

# Preface

So large has been the response to earlier editions of *America's Wonderful Little Hotels and Inns* that this, the fourth edition, appears in two volumes, one for travelers east of the Mississippi, the other for those visiting the West. The reason for this surge of enthusiasm for these special places to stay is not hard to find.

America is caught up in an innkeeping revolution. From quiet Texas border towns or the California wine country through the Midwest to the oldest and largest East Coast cities, travelers of all kinds—business people as well as vacationers—are seeking, and now finding, small hotels of character with the kind of grace and personalized service that the age of the motel and big chain hotel had all but consigned to history. In a new age of restoration and rediscovery of our varied but uniquely American past, all kinds of interesting buildings are getting new lives as hotels and inns. Some of them were historic townhouses or abandoned stately homes, a couple were general stores, several were boarding schools, at least one or two were brothels, hundreds were roadside taverns gone to seed.

Everyone seems to like these American classics: couples find romantic settings, business people value the quiet dignity and class, children can experience a kind of live-in history they will remember more vividly than a visit to any museum. Americans, innkeepers say, are more willing to make trade-offs to enjoy these old-fashioned luxuries. They are more willing to share bathrooms with other guests. They are content to put on a sweater and pull a chair closer to the fire if the heating becomes unreliable. They have found there is life without room service. "People want to see a little bit of how it used to be," said Harry Cregar, who rescued and restored the nineteenth-century canalside Riegelsville Hotel in historic Bucks County, Pennsylvania.

This new American innkeeping tradition, which is already challenging the reputation of European hotels, had its roots in the age of alternatives—the 1960s and 1970s—when Americans discovered restoration and urban renewal. Snatching up buildings that had been deserted or neglected in the rush to the suburban shopping malls, a new generation of innkeepers brought to these structures the fabrics, paints, and furniture that testify to the lead the United States has taken in interior design as well as in historic preservation. And they did more: they returned to cooking "from scratch," but with a sophistication that now supports a country full of fine food and wine shops. And the glorious breakfasts! There is probably nothing in the world of travel now to rival the best of the American inns' country-style breakfasts, with fresh fruit and juices, imaginative egg dishes, home-baked breads, and the best coffees and teas.

American innkeepers are as varied as the hotels and inns they run. Old people run inns; second-career people run inns; grown-up flower children run inns. Many successful innkeepers are women. Friends and couples of every description are in the business; sometimes whole families get into the spirit. Now and then the person who greets you at the door or brings you a cup of tea is a very small person indeed. The inn cat might spend the night in your armchair. Your innkeeper may be a musician, a painter, or the scion of the family in whose aristocratic home you are sleeping. At the Quimper Inn in Port Townsend, Washington, Paolo Wein and Mariii Lockwood are, among other things, jugglers. "On rainy days," Paolo says.

No state or Canadian province is without at least a handful of interesting places to stay, and the hotels are as diverse as the places they originally sprang up to serve. Want to sample a stagecoach stop? Try the 17-room Hotel Wolf in Saratoga, Wyoming. Want a college town hotel with Western glamour? Stay at Boulder, Colorado's ornate Boulderado. In Keosauqua, Iowa, there is the steamboat-stop Hotel Manning on the banks of the Des Moines River. In Natchez, Mississippi, you can stay in a former bawdy house in notorious Silver Street. Antebellum homes, gristmills, hunting lodges, spas, railway hostels, a lighthouse in Florida, a coffee plantation in Puerto Rico—the story of America is there to sample as you make your way around the country, eating and sleeping in local history instead of just looking at it from behind a velvet rope.

## HOW TO USE THIS BOOK

Because *America's Wonderful Little Hotels and Inns* is a collection of places with special character and interest, it is not intended to be a comprehensive nuts-and-bolts guide; nor is it a guide with inspectors and a rating system. The "experts" who wrote this book are the travelers themselves, along with a few local historians, architects, and specialists in preservation and restoration who are aware of how important this boom in innkeeping is to keeping alive a traditional America, with all its regional differences.

Individualists choose individualistic hotels and inns, so your tastes and needs may differ from those of one or more of the books' contributors. If they do—or if a place you try seems no longer to meet the description you read here—please write, so that other travelers can learn from your experience. This book can only grow and change if you, the reader, join in. Inns that draw a number of complaints are removed from the book's next edition. A historical building is not much comfort to the weary if the service is poor; and one person's quirky or talkative innkeeper may be another person's bore.

Information at the foot of each entry is provided by the innkeepers, who may forget now and then to include a detail or two that would make the difference to you. Write or telephone and ask about it. Bar and dining room services vary considerably among small hotels and inns, sometimes in response to the plethora of state and local laws governing the serving of food and alcohol, sometimes because of the size of an inn or its staff. Many small inns and hotels, however, are very cooperative and will, with a little notice, make special provisions for people with special needs. An increasing number of innkeepers are, for example, providing vegetarian food and some facilities for the handicapped. And if a small inn or hotel does not accept credit cards, it will very frequently take personal checks.

Most hotels and inns in this book charge by the room—or, increasingly, for a room and breakfast, though the practice is still far from universal. Where the full or modified American plan is in operation, the charge, which includes meals, is usually per person. But this can vary, so be certain to confirm your plan when booking your room. Ask also about state or local taxes, or service charges that may be added to your bill. Many small hotels and inns, incidentally, require advance booking and may ask for a deposit. Some of the more popular inns can be booked up at peak holiday times— Christmas, for example—for months or even a year in advance.

Like their companion, *Europe's Wonderful Little Hotels and Inns,* these volumes that comprise *America's Wonderful Little Hotels and Inns* owe their existence to many people. Each year the loyal corps of contributors grows—some of them have followings of their own because they have become recognizable names to be trusted by other readers who share their tastes. Each new edition brings adjustments; in this fourth edition, a larger number of inns have been dropped than from any earlier edition. This testifies to both the increasing discrimination of American travelers and the larger choice of interesting places to stay. A few hotels and inns continue to be the subject of controversy, and sometimes conflicting views are presented here because not all of us react the same way to places not stamped from molds.

As always, this book is dedicated gratefully to the generous, wise, and witty people who wrote it.

# *Part One*

## Far West and Hawaii

*Arizona*
*California*
*Hawaii*
*Nevada*
*Utah*

# Arizona

## Cochise

**The Cochise Hotel**
Cochise, Arizona 85606
Telephone (602) 384-3156

"This isolated, remotely situated hotel was built when the railroad was in its heyday. It is a place for those who enjoy solitude. The place is filled with antiques; every room is different. Mrs. Harrington prepares home-cooked meals. She tells you when to be at the family-style table—and you had better be there! This hotel is unknown by most people, and those who do know it prefer it that way."
—*John Doty*

"Meals are put on the table and guests eat family style. Reservations are required because Mrs. Harrington broils chicken and steak (for both lunch and dinner) according to the number of orders. If guests aren't there at noon or at 6 o'clock sharp for meals, the food will get cold."
—*JLS*

Open 2 weeks, then closed 4 days, then open 2 weeks, etc., all year. Call ahead.
3 rooms, 2 suites, all with private bath.

Rates $14 single, $17 double, $26 suites.
No credit cards.
Owner: Elizabeth Husband.

---

## _Grand Canyon_

### El Tovar Hotel
Grand Canyon, Arizona 86023
Telephone (602) 638-2631

"At the decidedly abrupt edge of the southern rim of the Grand Canyon, at Bright Angel's Point, is this small hotel, which is something of a lodge. Despite that identification, it is a very grand place in the manner that a Teddy Roosevelt would appreciate. Canyon limestone and ponderosa pine logs make up its structure. Its facade is abutted by a vast front porch with a seemingly endless line of comfortable chairs arranged for maximum viewing of the canyon. Inside, its great hall is dominated by one of the most vast chimneypieces ever conceived. The rooms are ample, if somewhat rustic, and strenuously punctuated by the rhythmic insistency of the steam heat in the early morning hours. El Tovar's food and drink—done in the tradition of the Santa Fe Railroad's Harvey Girls—are of high quality. The wine list, too, is probably one of the better ones in the Southwest.

"El Tovar has always attracted a worldly society. Vita Sackville-West spent a fair time in residence at the lodge during World War II and celebrated it in a moving if episodic book recalling her life 'hibernating by the rim.' Scores of her fellow Britishers have followed, undoubtedly attracted by the drama of her tome. The rooms, with their ample mullioned windows and their splendid view, have inspired some of the great artists and photographers. One European diplomat said that El Tovar was one of America's great landmarks. I think him right. In a sense it serves as a chronicle of the Southwest from the days of the 'noble savage' to those of the Anglo rancher. El Tovar is used by all—artist, traveler, rancher, and local."

—_Dr. F. M. Hinkhouse_

Open all year.
78 rooms, all with private bath.
Rates $63–$110.
Credit cards: American Express, Carte Blanche, Diners Club, MasterCard, Visa.
Grand Canyon National Park airport has connecting flights to Phoenix and Las Vegas. Bus service to park from Flagstaff, Phoenix, and Las Vegas.
Manager: Toby Allen.

# Litchfield Park

**The Wigwam**
Litchfield Park, Arizona 85340
Telephone: (602) 935-3811

"The Wigwam is a resort hotel and country club with three golf courses rated among the top 100 in the country. It also has two swimming pools, eight tennis courts, and a riding stable. The four-star restaurant is super. A wonderful place, quiet unless you go with a group, with lots of opportunities for the sports loving. The place is very casual except for dinner. Be sure to reserve well in advance. At Christmas time it can take a year to get a reservation. We keep going back!"                                          *—Wally Laster*

Open mid-September through May.
225 rooms, all with private bath and patio.
Rates $174–$184 double, AP. Special packages available, including
   golf, tennis, and horseback riding.
No credit cards.
Four-star restaurant/bar.
Innkeeper: Clark Corbett.

# Paradise Valley

**Hermosa Inn**
5532 North Palo Cristi Road
Paradise Valley, Arizona 85253
Telephone (602) 955-8660

Lon Megargee, a cowboy artist, built this rambling hacienda in 1930, guided by inspiration and, the story goes, without formal blueprints. He had then completed some paintings for the Arizona State Capitol; he later became better known for his paintings called *Black Bart* and *Cowboy's Dream.* When Megargee decided to move on, the building he left behind became a guest ranch. Much of the original structure is still there: the beehive fireplaces, the secret passages, and huge doors.

"The inn has a resort feeling within what could be considered metropolitan Phoenix. The fun and pleasures of the city's restaurants, museums, and shopping areas are only minutes away by car. Yet the inn is in a residential area, which creates a noncommercial atmosphere. Although rooms have been added, the charm of the old home remains. There is a delightful dining room where good food and a fireplace (with a fire in season) add to the ambience. The grounds are magnificently landscaped in the cactus and rock motif typical of the area. There are tennis courts for those who insist on activity, and a pool that is part of the lovely setting. One of the most pleasurable experiences is staying in a *casita,* a small apartment where one can enjoy a quiet breakfast overlooking the desert garden. From the inn, Camelback Mountain is clearly and magnificently present."                                                  —*Muriel Burnstein*

Open all year.
25 rooms, all with private bath.
Rates $48 single, $72 double.
Credit cards: American Express, Diners Club, MasterCard, Visa.
French, German, Italian, and Spanish spoken.
Innkeeper: Mary Locoro.

## Phoenix

### Arizona Biltmore
24th Street and Missouri
Phoenix, Arizona 85016
Telephone (602) 955-6600

"Arizona Biltmore is the original desert resort created by that most sensitive master of desert architects, Frank Lloyd Wright. Since its inception in the thirties and through modernization and expansion by younger architects at the Frank Lloyd Wright Foundation, it has maintained the highest standards of service and cuisine."
                                                  —*George Herzog*

Open all year.
505 rooms, all with private bath.
Rates $130–$190 single, $155–$215 double. Summer rates: $60–$80 single, $70–$90 double.
Credit cards: American Express, Carte Blanche, Diners Club, MasterCard, Visa.
Manager: Cecil Ravenswood.

## Scottsdale

### The Inn at McCormick Ranch
7401 North Scottsdale Road
Scottsdale, Arizona 85253
Telephone (602) 948-5050

"The Inn at McCormick Ranch is not typically Arizonan. It is a green oasis in the desert. While many other resorts emphasize Western atmosphere, McCormick features rolling lawns shaded with numerous trees and a lake. It is almost like a transplanted Eastern inn, although the architecture of the buildings is Mexican-Western. We had a very spacious corner suite overlooking the lake and enjoyed the privacy of a small balcony—privacy, that is, if you don't count the ducks, geese, and a lone pelican who adopted us after we shared our breakfast with them. There are sailboats and pedal boats on the lake, and fishing equipment can be rented if you wish to try your luck. There is a swimming pool near the bar and restaurant. The only complaint I would have is that there were not enough umbrellas near the pool for redheads like me, who burn to a crisp without beneficial shade.

"The food is good, and the service, by a very young staff, is smiling, courteous, and efficient. Try the bison steak—a different and quite palatable experience. The inn has a small boutique where you will find all that you have forgotten at home. And—a nice touch —the lady who runs the place will ask you if you wish to reserve a newspaper since they sell out very quickly. She will save it for you and it will be brought up to your room with your breakfast tray."

—*Louisa L. Becker*

"The great pleasures of the inn are the stunning mountain view offered by many rooms, and breakfast outdoors by the lake. Unfortunately, the cooking is uneven and the service not quite in league with the prices. I think it is overrated." —*George Herzog*

Open all year.
125 rooms, all with private bath.
Rates mid-January–end of April: rooms $120–$130, suites $200–$350; May 1–May 27: rooms $80–$95, suites $175–$300; May 28–September 30: rooms $50–$60, suites $100–$150; September–mid-January: rooms $85–$110, suites $225–$300.
Credit cards: American Express, Carte Blanche, Diners Club, MasterCard, Visa.
German and Spanish spoken.
Limousine service (about $5) available from Phoenix airport. Guests picked up free at Scottsdale airport. Trains and buses to Phoenix, 15 miles away.
Manager: John Daley.

All innkeepers appreciate reservations in advance; some require them.

_____ *Tucson*

**Arizona Inn**
2200 East Elm Street
Tucson, Arizona 85719
Telephone (602) 325-1541

"Every desert city, be it Marrakech or Tucson, has its oasis, its caravansary. Not too far from the heart of Tucson—and hard by the University of Arizona—is the Arizona Inn. Here, within a dozen acres, are immaculate gardens. The inn's dusty-pink walls, decidedly Andalusian in feeling, are elaborated with wood and iron grilles and endless cascades of flowers. Within the rooms are creature comforts that echo the taste of a more leisurely age. Lunch is served beside a cobalt-blue pool. The food is imaginative; an endless mosaic of salads tempts all but a diet-stricken Hollywood starlet. Dinner in the cathedral-ceilinged great hall is likely to be preceded by drinks in the adjacent cantina. The university provides a rich offering of concerts, exhibitions, and even planetary viewing in the recently completed observatory. Those doggedly searching for the exotic can take a run down to the nearby border town of Nogales, where fun and games are available for all tastes."

—*Dr. F. M. Hinkhouse*

"I agree with everything Dr. Hinkhouse says except for the 'imaginative food.' I found it (with the exception of delicious exotic salads) unenterprising, considering that this is a luxury hotel. Too many steaks of different varieties, frozen fish, bottled sauces, and a curious, sweet, pink concoction they call 'French dressing' but which bears no relation to its name. A small helping of anything was really difficult to come by and several waiters told me that what was left over was generally thrown away. This seems to be true in so many U.S. hotels, and it shocks me in a starving world."

—*Miranda Mackintosh*

Open all year.
85 rooms, all with private bath.
Rates $42–$95 single, $57–$105 double, depending on season.
Credit cards: American Express, Carte Blanche, MasterCard, Visa.
Spanish spoken.
Arizona Statecoach cab service meets planes at Tucson airport, 12
    miles away.
Managing Director: Robert Minerich.

Turn to the back of this book for pages inviting *your* comments.

---

## The Lodge on the Desert
306 North Alvernon Way (P.O. Box 42500)
Tucson, Arizona 85733
Telephone (602) 325-3366

"This is a sprawling combination of large Spanish-style rooms, many with beehive fireplaces. The center of the grounds is the pool area, which is beautifully landscaped and has a tranquil view of the mountains in the distance. Here is an oasis of peace and quiet right in the heart of the city—although sometimes you can hear traffic noise. The restaurant is very good. There are many pleasant diversions in the area, best of which is the natural beauty of the desert."
                                                        —*Muriel Burnstein*

Open all year.
38 rooms, 5 suites, all with private bath.
Rates $34–$90 single, $38–$102 double, including continental
    breakfast.
Credit cards: MasterCard, Visa.
Spanish spoken.
Airport limousine to inn. Tucson has a good public bus system.
Innkeeper: Schuyler W. Lininger.

Details of special features offered by an inn or hotel vary according to information supplied by the hotels themselves. The absence here of a recreational amenity, a bar, or a restaurant doesn't necessarily mean one of these doesn't exist. Ask the innkeeper when booking your room.

La Valencia Hotel,
La Jolla

# California

# Anchor Bay

**Whale Watch**
35100 Highway 1 (Box 127)
Anchor Bay, California 95445
Telephone (707) 884-3667

"Three hours (by car) north of San Francisco on scenic Highway 1, a new venture, Whale Watch, appeared a few years ago, offering an unmatched combination of scenery, privacy, and beautifully planned accommodations. From a quiet two-acre spot overlooking the Pacific visitors can watch the migration of gray whales and the work of a salmon fleet as it comes and goes from the harbor at Anchor Bay. The bay has a beach reached by a staircase within 100 feet of the condominium units at the cliffside inn, or you can view it from a private deck. There are restaurants in the vicinity, but guests can also choose to shop in Anchor Bay and cook in the fully equipped kitchens in Whale Watch suites."   —*Elnora S. Robinson*

"I agree with the recommendation concerning Whale Watch. The place combines comfort, privacy, and one of the most spectacular views in the world—a vacation for the mind, body, and spirit!"
—*Richard W. Cucco*

10

"It is quiet and peaceful, and on a moonlit night was the most gorgeous spot I've ever seen. The managers and owners have added special appointments with flowers, furnishings, first-grade beautiful linens, art, and the best in reading materials. After a visit here one must return again and again. The accommodation is superior."

—*Goldie Groseclose*

Open all year.
6 suites, all with private bath.
Rates $75–$105.
No credit cards.
Bus connections to Santa Rosa.
Innkeepers: Irene and Enoch Stewart.

_____*Aptos*

**Apple Lane Inn**
6265 Soquel Drive
Aptos, California 95003
Telephone (408) 475-6868

"An hour and a half down the coast from San Francisco—and what a spectacular coast it is—and ten minutes from the lovely town of Santa Cruz, is Apple Lane Inn. The driveway, not surprisingly, leads through an old apple orchard, and at the top is a Victorian farm-house—beige, with ornate white trim, light-blue shutters, and maroon accents. Here, in spring of 1983, after years of renovating, Barbara Buckmaster and Peter Farquhar opened a very pretty small inn—four rooms. The renovation was masterful. Everything is beautifully done—William Morris wallpapers, stenciled floors, antique furniture or unobtrusive reproductions.

"Two rooms up under the eaves share a pretty, well-appointed bath, with handsome brass fixtures and a tub with feet. Two other, larger bedrooms on the second floor have baths of their own. Coffee appears in an upstairs sitting room at 6:30 A.M., and it is from a phone in this room that one makes reservations at the many good restaurants in the vicinity—there is a thick book of sample menus to choose among. A good continental breakfast is served in the bay-windowed parlor, and Mr. Farquhar, a geographer at Cabrillo College (which is nearby and has a track for joggers), can be persuaded, afterward, to show you his first edition of Hakluyt's *Voyages* or his signed and numbered edition of Stanley's *In Darkest Africa.*

"After a day beside the Pacific or among the redwoods, one goes down to the Cider Room, where the guests assemble for darts and homemade cider. Or one can sit out on the brick terrace and have a drink amid roses, giant geraniums, calla lilies, lemon trees, and a showy shrub called Australian tea, covered with bright red blossoms. Not to mention Acadia and Monterey pine.

"This is not really a full-fledged inn, but it is far more comfortable and gracious than the ordinary bed-and-breakfast operation. A charming stopover in a lovely part of the world."

*—Tom Congdon*

Open all year.
4 rooms, 2 with private bath.
Rate $60, including continental breakfast.
Credit cards: MasterCard, Visa.
Proprietors: Peter Farquhar and Barbara Buckmaster.

# Beverly Hills

## L'Ermitage
9291 Burton Way
Beverly Hills, California 90210
Telephone (213) 278-3344

"It is beautiful, it is quiet, old-fashioned, gracious, and elegant with touches that almost all over the world disappeared with World War II—and you can really call it a hotel. It has no rooms, only suites, all beautifully appointed. There are no convention crowds, no noisy groups, no boisterous guests. The street is almost like one in Paris with its trees, boutiques, and sidewalks wide enough and safe enough to take a stroll. The restaurant serves excellent food and is for the exclusive use of hotel guests. If you prefer room service, you will receive hot food, beautifully presented and graciously served. There is a fireplace in your suite, you are given a daily newspaper, and if you leave your shoes at your door (oh, French hotels of my youth revisited!), they will be polished before you wake. That *ne plus ultra* is L'Ermitage."

*—Louisa L. Becker*

"Well, it wasn't quite like a street in Paris. There were few trees and very little traffic, even though it was a six-lane boulevard. But L'Ermitage is a superior place. Suites have kitchenettes and sitting rooms and such, arranged in a long space cleverly divided by partial walls, railings, and transparent drapery that allows air into a balcony sleeping area (one step up)."

*—Camille J. Cook*

Open all year.
114 suites, all with private bath.
Rates $145–$765, including continental breakfast.

Credit cards: American Express, Carte Blanche, Diners Club, MasterCard, Visa.
Manager: Reinhold Engelmann.

_____*Big Sur*

**The Ventana Inn**
California Highway 1
Big Sur, California 93920
Telephone (408) 667-2331; 624-4812

"Ventana, perched on a ridge of the coastal mountains bearing the same name, is an environment that celebrates its magnificent situation with endlessly ramified forests on one side and the limitless Pacific on the other.

"The bar and restaurant are capacious, done in low-keyed yet psychologically warm tones that force the guest's eye beyond to the sea and to the mountains. From them, presumably, one receives strength. Banquettes are upholstered in handsome Oriental rugs and heavily textured stuff.

"After a Lucullan repast, the guest is delighted to stroll through the copse to his quarters. There, all is wonderfully quiet except for the tranquilizing murmur of the wind in the pines. The extraordinarily commodious rooms lend themselves to quiet comfort and reflection. The cares of the city seem light years away and sleep comes easily. In the morning a breakfast tray can be brought to your room, where you may elect to enjoy it on your balcony overlooking the land Robinson Jeffers so loved and heralded in his verse.

"If you prefer, you can go to the morning room and enjoy your juice, brioche, and coffee with other guests. Chances are, however, that they may be reading a book while they sip their coffee. Ventana, in the final analysis, is a very private place."

—*Dr. F. M. Hinkhouse*

"The Ventana Inn, set on the side of a hill in the sheltering woods across the road from the drama of the Big Sur coast, is in complete harmony with the surrounding wilderness. The separate structures have the clean, natural lines and casual community that we Easterners associate with the California spirit. Each suite has blond wood walls, a private porch, and brightly colored quilts that match the crafted headboards. Even the soap is true to the naturalness of the whole. Breakfast is shared by all the guests around the fire in the main house. A neighboring general store offers local wine (not especially recommended) and Monterey Jack cheese for picnics on the beach."                                      —*Laura Rose Handman*

"There must be a reason why the windows of the cottages don't look out on the spectacular ocean view, but we don't know what it is. It's the only quibble we can make. The Ventana is marvelous. Someone should shyly mention that the bathhouse, open until 2 A.M., is a pretty sexy place, with private men's and women's pools feeding into a common pool under the stars. Who knows when somebody gorgeous might paddle over?"                   —*Tom Congdon*

"An altogether lovely place. The rooms don't look like much from the outside, but they are exceptionally well designed and decorated. Few rooms have ocean views but the view from the pool is nice. Breakfasts are generous, with lots of fresh fruit and a rich assortment of brioches, croissants, and homemade fruit loaves. The hotel offers its residents fresh fruit and coffee free throughout the day, and wine and French cheeses between 4 and 6 P.M. The staff is very friendly. The only complaint is that the rooms are poorly insulated."                                         —*Hilary Rubinstein*

Open all year.
40 rooms, all with private bath, 2 with private hot tubs.
Rates $125–$300 double, including breakfast.
Credit cards: American Express, Diners Club, MasterCard, Visa.
Some French and Italian spoken.
Bus service from Monterey.
Innkeeper: Randy Smith.

_____*Boyes Hot Springs*

**Sonoma Mission Inn**
18140 Sonoma Highway (Box I)
Boyes Hot Springs, California 95416
Telephone (707) 996-1041

"The Hispanic-style Sonoma Mission Inn, hard by a lovely creek that wends its way through the property and backed by a dramatic growth of redwood trees extending partway up the piedmontlike hills, has been restored and given a new life.

"The inn reminds one of a small, understated, and well-decorated microcosm of the Beverly Hills Hotel. The Great Hall, grand and elegant, establishes the mood, the image of the hotel. The Provençal Restaurant could not be more tasteful in any sense. The splendidly understated Grill is dominated by a pianist who knows the world of Cole Porter decidedly well; it is the right venue to enjoy the local wines and salads from local gardens. The rooms, executed in taupe, coffee, and terra cotta, are ideal for relaxation, slumber, and sleep. All are near the giant pool with its chalk-white cabanas, and the Spa. As an English lady of "a certain age" said to me, "This is certainly a hotel to reckon with!"        —*Dr. F. M. Hinkhouse*

Open all year.
100 rooms, all with private bath.
Rates, package plan only, from $50 per person per night, including continental breakfast, bottle of wine, and use of Spa.
Credit cards: All accepted.
French, German, and Spanish spoken.
Innkeeper: Jill S. Cury.

_____*Calistoga*

**Mountain Home Ranch**
3400 Mountain Home Ranch Road
Calistoga, California 94515
Telephone (707) 942-6616

"Nestled in a secluded canyon, Mountain Home Ranch offers hospitality and fine food to visitors to the Napa Valley. To those wishing to savor the products of the bountiful vineyards of this famous wine-growing region and to those wishing to luxuriate in the natural hot spring spas of Calistoga, Mountain Home Ranch provides an excellent base from which to take daily tours.

"Mountain Home Ranch was established as a family resort hotel in 1914 on the original ranch homestead of Ludwig and Emma Orth, who came to northern California from Germany. Accommodations are available in the main lodge or in secluded cabins spread about the ranch property."        —*Robert L. Hanelt*

"I stayed in a rustic cabin at the ranch, and it was reminiscent of childhood camps. Mountain Home provided a most restful stay. It is perfect for children."        —*Phyllis Faber Kelley*

"The trails that wander through the property to lakes and streams are a respite from the average accommodations and a delight for the family. Though a central spot for touring, it is not necessary to leave the ranch if you just wish to relax and enjoy nature at its best."
        —*Mr. and Mrs. R. L. Tucker*

Open February through December.
24 rooms, 16 with private bath.
Rates $28–$77, including continental breakfast.

Credit cards: MasterCard, Visa.
French spoken.
Greyhound bus to Calistoga; guests met.
Innkeeper: Roberta Leonard.

---

## Wine Way Inn
1019 Foothill Boulevard
Calistoga, California 94515
Telephone (707) 942-0680

"The Wine Way Inn is one of the nicest places you could stay in. So clean. We had a little apartment in the back—not attached to the house, but with a private bath. Breakfast is served in the main house —homemade breads, fruit, and coffee. Nearby is the Roman Spa, and many wineries are within a short drive."   —*Lila Haberman*

Open February through November.
5 rooms, 1 cottage, 4 private baths.
Rates $60–$75 per room per night, including continental breakfast
   with homemade pastries.
Credit cards: MasterCard, Visa.
Innkeepers: Allen and Dede Good.

---

## *Carmel*

"Quaint" is the word most often used by tourists to describe Carmel. Lovely homes, comfortable inns, interesting boutiques, and windblown trees cling to the slope that leads to the sea. The beach is spectacular, with the finest, whitest sand in the world. But watch the water; the undertow can be treacherous and unexpected at times.

---

## Cypress Inn
Lincoln and Seventh (P.O. Box Y)
Carmel, California 93921
Telephone (408) 624-3871

"The Cypress Inn is operated by the same people who manage the Pine Inn, also in Carmel. It has very elegant Spanish-style public

rooms, but limited accommodations for your car. Get into the official parking lot early or be prepared to keep moving every two hours to stay ahead of the Carmel police. The parking nuisance is compensated for by your being in the thick of things. You are just a half-block from the main drag (Junipero Avenue), which is lined with shops of every description: high-fashion clothing, California crafts, wine-and-cheese delis for your picnic lunches, and galleries that offer 'safe' paintings. Restaurants are a problem, often overcrowded on weekends and not up to gourmet standards. Don't miss hiking in the Point Lobos State Reserve for knock-your-socks-off scenic interest. To rubberneck in the high-rent district, pay the toll to take the seventeen-mile drive. Nice rooms at the Cypress are even better if you get a balcony (215Q and 217Q are two with that feature)."
—*Camille J. Cook*

"The place has a friendly air. It is true that the hotel's own car park only has room for eight cars, but it is quite close to a residential area with no parking restrictions. The rooms facing the back are adequate but a bit claustrophobic."          —*Hilary Rubinstein*

Open all year.
33 rooms, all with private bath.
Rates $45–$75, including continental breakfast.
Credit cards: American Express, MasterCard, Visa.
Manager: Robert A. Davey.

---

**Happy Landing Inn**
Monte Verde between 5th and 6th (Box 2619)
Carmel, California 93921
Telephone (408) 624-7917

"Innkeepers Bob Alberson and Dick Stewart gave my wife and me the most gracious and enjoyable service of our recent trip. We can't say enough good things about this inn in downtown Carmel. The homemade breakfast served in our room was very special. We stayed an extra three days, and can't wait for our next visit."
—*Bill Adams*

Open all year.
5 rooms, all with private bath; 2 suites with shared bath.
Rates $45–$65.
Credit cards: American Express, MasterCard, Visa.
Innkeepers: Dick Stewart and Bob Alberson.

---

## Normandy Inn
P.O. Box 1706
Carmel, California 93921
Telephone (408) 624-3825

"Carmel is an enchanting area divided by Ocean Avenue with its cypresses, groups of rhododendrons, and other colorful flowers in season. On either side of the avenue are small shops, packed closely together. There is a clean, sandy beach where children and dogs run freely, joggers take their daily exercise, families picnic, enthusiastic surfers enjoy their sport, and sandcastles are built in competition. Only a few blocks east of the ocean—and within easy walking distance of a concert hall, a theater, a movie house, innumerable art galleries and restaurants—stands the Normandy Inn. The front steps are decorated with blooming flowers. The walk leading to the newer rooms is lined with potted geraniums, and beyond that is a garden patio with easy chairs and a heated swimming pool. Just across the side street are two cottages with enclosed patios. The main office is small, neat, unpretentious. Adjoining it is the breakfast room, where a fine continental breakfast is served. In the Normandy-style section of the inn, around a courtyard, are double rooms with bathrooms, well-furnished tiny kitchens, and a dressing area with mirrors and drawers. Some of the double rooms have fireplaces in addition to steam heat, where hearth fires, if needed, are laid daily with wood provided by the management. Having traveled abroad and in this country I have chosen to return to Normandy for many years because I consider it a most unusual place to stay for a few weeks." —*Frederica Mitchell; also recommended by Robert Hochhauser*

"This must be the most overrated place in town. I think it is resting on its laurels." —*Camille J. Cook*

Open all year.
45 rooms, 3 houses, all with private bath.
Rates $54–$62 single, $59–$67 double, $91–$98 suites, $101–$122 cottages, including continental breakfast.
No credit cards.
Innkeeper: Samuel M. Stanton.


Do you know a hotel in your state that we have overlooked? Write *now*.

## Pine Inn
Ocean Avenue between Lincoln and Monte Verde (Box
250)
Carmel, California 93921
Telephone (408) 624-3851

"This turn-of-the-century inn, which still maintains its Victorian
flavor, is on busy Ocean Avenue. Always good, with a charming
atmosphere, and right in the heart of Carmel for those who like to
wander through the shops and art galleries."
*—Mrs. Bartley M. Harloe*

"Pine Inn may be the class act in town. Penthouse suites are spectacular." *—Camille J. Cook*

"We didn't care for the look of this place despite its central position
in the shopping part of town. The lobby was very crowded with a
group of travelers." *—Hilary Rubinstein*

Open all year.
49 rooms, all with private bath.
Rates $50–$110.
Credit cards: American Express, MasterCard, Visa.
Limousine service from Monterey airport, minibus from Salinas
    railway station.
Innkeepers: Max and Carroll McKee.

## San Antonio House
P.O. Box 3683
Carmel, California 93921
Telephone (408) 624-4334

" 'A garret for young lovers' insists on coming to mind when I
search for a description of the rooms we occupied in the attic of the
San Antonio House. Our suite was a red, black, and white decorating triumph. A nondescript bench is raised to 'artistic accent' by the
application of red enamel and the addition of patchwork-covered
pillows. Bits of black-and-white wallpaper adorn triangular sections
of wall under the dormers. A collection of prints, drawings, and
photos of Venice (including some of snow-rimmed canals) presents
an evocative touch in California. Marimekko sheets and quilts

brighten the two bedrooms. You can't stand up in the bathtub (those eaves again) but it makes no difference if you are young at heart and there to enjoy the glories of the Monterey Peninsula. Your hideout is equipped with your own coffeepot and a refrigerator stocked with orange juice. (And you are just one block from the softest white sand I have ever touched.) I saw one other suite (above the garage) in the San Antonio House complex and felt it did not come up to the 'charm quotient' of our place. Be specific when you reserve."

—*Camille J. Cook*

Open all year.
4 suites, all with private bath.
Rates $55–$65.
No credit cards.
Italian and Spanish spoken.
Innkeepers: Michael and Joan Cloran.

---

## The Sandpiper Inn
2408 Bayview Avenue at Martin
Carmel, California 93923
Telephone (408) 624-6433

"We had a lovely room overlooking the spendid Carmel beach— very light and airy. The owners, who are Scottish, were very friendly, but the place has a slight guesthouse feel to it. A large television set in the main public room tended to inhibit conversation."

—*Hilary Rubinstein*

"This one is for lovers of isolation, though it is on a residential street. It's a hefty walk to town, where all the action is."

—*Camille J. Cook*

Open all year.
15 rooms and cottages, all with private bath.
Rates $55–$90, including continental breakfast.
Credit cards: MasterCard, Visa.
French, German, and Italian spoken.
Air and Greyhound bus service to Monterey, railroad to Salinas.
Innkeepers: Graeme and Irene Mackenzie.

Where are the good little hotels in Boston? Philadelphia? Omaha? Dallas? If you have found one, don't keep it a secret. Write *now*.

## Sea View Inn
Camino Real between 11th and 12th Streets (Box 4138)
Carmel, California 93921
Telephone (408) 624-8778

"The small town of Carmel is really an enchanted village full of craft shops, European-style eateries, and homes whose owners very cleverly translate even the smallest yard into an elegant and private garden. The inn, a restored Victorian house, offers the traveler a special experience in lodging and is definitely not for those who prefer large color television sets over the quiet sounds of the village and nearby Pacific Ocean. The inn is owned and managed by the Hydorn family, all natives of California, who go out of their way to make each guest's stay pleasant and comfortable. Each of the eight guest rooms has its own enchanting decor, and a sprinkling of antiques adds a feeling of quaint security and stability to the establishment. Continental breakfast, accompanied by fresh California fruits and juices, is served at the fireside in the front parlor every morning; and, in the evenings, there are sherry and port."
    —*Susan M. Lee Bales; also recommended by Camille J. Cook*

Open all year.
8 rooms, 6 with private bath.
Rates $40–$60, including continental breakfast.
Credit cards: MasterCard, Visa.
French spoken.
20 minutes from Monterey airport; airport limousine service. Greyhound bus service to Monterey with connecting local service.
Innkeepers: Marshall and Diane Hydorn.

## Vagabond House
P.O. Box 2747
Fourth and Dolores Streets
Carmel, California 93921
Telephone (408) 624-7738

"Carmel-by-the-Sea began at the turn of the century as a colony for artists and a summer home for the affluent residents of San Francisco. Over the years the area has been home to Robinson Jeffers,

John Steinbeck, Fernand Léger, Alexander Archipenko, and Ansel Adams. Carmel is known for its fine restaurants, unique inns, artists' studios, and unusual shops.

"Nestled in this gorgeous piece of real estate is Vagabond House. Service at the Vagabond is as extraordinary as its scenery. Errands are run for you, free transportation to and from Monterey airport arranged, dinner reservations obtained, unlimited logs and free coffee supplied—these are just some of the ways the Vagabond spoils its guests. Fresh flowers and fruit welcome guests, and the rooms are filled with original artworks and antiques from all over the United States."  *—Truman and Ver Jean Chaffin*

"No description would be complete without a mention of the flag-stone courtyard that all the rooms face. Old and very large live oak trees occupy the center, and these are adorned with hanging baskets of fuchsias, tuberous begonias, ferns, and many other plants. Camellias, rhododendrons, and azaleas circle the trees, and each room and balcony has its own plantings of flowers and greenery. Squirrels that chatter through the branches of the oaks are fed each morning from the office."  *—Grace A. Bixby*

"The flowers are beautiful, the accommodations immaculate."  *—Phyllis Faber Kelley*

"The Vagabond House has the most delightful setting of any of the inns I've seen in Carmel. The cluster of units set on a hill around the courtyard is very simpatico. A top choice for Carmel visitors."  *—Camille J. Cook*

"The room they showed me was in the back and a bit poky. I also felt that the ground-floor rooms overlooking the courtyard lacked privacy. Prices are reasonable, though."  *—Hilary Rubinstein*

Open all year.
12 rooms, all with private bath.
Rates $50–$85, including continental breakfast.
Credit cards: MasterCard, Visa.
Monterey Peninsula bus service.
Innkeeper: Bruce Indorato.

_____ *Cloverdale*

**Vintage Towers**
302 North Main Street
Cloverdale, California 95425
Telephone (707) 894-4535

"Two things set Vintage Towers far above any of the other bed-and-breakfast places that have opened recently in this area. First is the elegant charm of the stately old mansion itself, and second (perhaps more important) is the wonderful hospitality of the owners, Tom and Judy Haworth. They will invite you to share a glass of wine with them in the library; their conversation is stimulating, their enthusiasm for their home is a delight, and their desire as hosts to meet your needs is warm and genuine."    —*Carol Glen*

Open all year.
7 rooms, 3 tower suites, 4 with private bath.
Rates $35–$65, including full breakfast.
Credit cards: MasterCard, Visa.
Some French and Italian spoken.
3 blocks to Greyhound terminal.
Innkeepers: Tom and Judy Haworth.

_____*Columbia*

**City Hotel**
Main Street (Box 1870)
Columbia, California 95310
Telephone (209) 532-1479

"Columbia as a town is a fascinating daguerreotype of the past: quaint, isolated, and frozen into the late gold rush era of the Sierra foothills. The City Hotel is a wooden-verandaed brick-fronted building stretching back into the 1850s. It has been completely restored with a dining room lighted with period fixtures, frontier saloon, and upstairs bedrooms furnished in old Victorian style with polished brass bedsteads, cuspidors, pitcher-basin washstands, beveled lead-glass mirrors, and all the trimmings, including modern plumbing and lighting conveniences as well.

"But charming though it is as a wayside inn, it is the dining room that will, in my mind, earn the City Hotel its greatest claim to fame. Barry Marcillac, chef for many years at one of San Francisco's most renowned restaurants, is a master at his trade. I have never tasted more delectable vegetables *en croute,* more delicate soufflés, or more excellently prepared wilted-spinach salad. I am something of an amateur cook myself and can usually at least match the quality of the restaurants in which I eat, but I have yet to come near the cuisine of this one. The wine list, too, is unique in that it is exclusively California's best, and chosen only from small, family-owned wineries. I know of no better selection anywhere. The service is impeccable and the decor is demure. While I am loath to give away one of my few remaining secret hideaways in California, I also feel talent and hard work deserve recognition and applause. I tip my glass to the City Hotel!"                                   —*Harold J. Seger*

Open all year.
9 rooms, all with half-bath.
Rates $55.50–$57.50, including continental breakfast.
Credit cards: MasterCard, Visa.
Yosemite Airlines serves Columbia airport. Greyhound buses to Sonora, 3 miles away.
Innkeeper: Tom Bender.

## *Coronado*

**Hotel del Coronado**
1500 Orange Avenue
Coronado, California 92118
Telephone (714) 435-6611

"This hotel, though now much enlarged, has atmosphere and old-fashioned charm. It also has historical interest: the Prince of Wales, later Edward VIII and the Duke of Windsor, stayed here, and the dinner service for the prince is on display in one of the vitrines. Wallis Simpson also was a frequent visitor at the time her husband was an officer at the naval base on Coronado—no, their paths did not cross then! Other illustrious guests have spent time at the hotel. Some old rooms have dated plumbing, which even leaks, but all in all it is a gracious old lady worthy of mentioning."
—*Louisa L. Becker*

"A Victorian seaside fancy, replete with turrets! The Hotel Del, as its friends affectionately call it, has been the scene of many movies, but of even more memorable dinners. The principal dining salons offer a very fine standard of traditional continental cooking under a stunningly beautiful vaulted wood ceiling. Rooms are available in both new and old buildings, which appear to be well maintained."
—*George Herzog*

Open all year.
686 rooms scattered among several buildings, all rooms with private bath.
Rates $68–$525.
Credit cards: American Express, Carte Blanche, Diners Club, MasterCard, Visa.

Many languages spoken.
Manager: Scott W. Anderson.

_____*Eureka*

## The Eureka Inn
7th and F Streets
Eureka, California 95501
Telephone (707) 442-6441

"The pluperfect time to be a guest in this tidy pseudo-Tudor lodge, hard by the Pacific, is Christmas. Its Great Hall, dominated by a Paul Bunyanesque fireplace, is further decorated with all the impedimenta of the Yule season. It is the ideal family retreat for the Christmas season. The inn has a handsome dining room that features the fruits of the nearby sea—something not to be missed. Adjacent is a coffee shop that is a lair for local lawyers, loggers, and the gentry from the Redwood Empire. Needless to say, the decor of the inn is a handsome reflection of its ambience—as is to be expected. After all, it was built by a major timber family who wanted to have a place to entertain—not a bad approach, not a bad idea, especially when it is done with such singular good taste."

—*Dr. F. M. Hinkhouse*

Open all year.
95 rooms and 15 suites, all with private bath.
Rates $42–$52 single, $56–$70 double, $80–$250 suites.
Credit cards: American Express, Carte Blanche, Diners Club, MasterCard, Visa.
Manager: John Porter.

_____*Ferndale*

## The Gingerbread Mansion
400 Berding Street
Ferndale, California 95536
Telephone (707) 786-4000

"This is undoubtedly the most luxurious inn we've ever found. It is beautifully decorated in the Victorian manner, boasting comfortable antique beds, lovely bedding, extra large, thick towels, and bathrooms that defy description. Innkeeper Wendy Hatfield believes in pampering her guests with such niceties as attractive bathrobes in each room, fresh flowers everywhere, and early morning coffee or tea outside the room to sustain you while she prepares an ample breakfast of fresh fruit and cheese and a variety of home-baked breads.

"The town of Ferndale, twenty minutes from Eureka, is a Victorian village which impressed us with its neatness and friendliness. The shopping center was a refreshing change from the hundreds of boutiques encountered elsewhere. We found the wares a little different and the prices reasonable."        —*Tom and Marian Francis*

Open all year.
4 rooms, 2 with private sink, 1 with woodburning stove, all sharing baths.
Rates $45–$65, including breakfast and afternoon tea and cake.
Credit cards: MasterCard, Visa.
French, Portuguese, Spanish, and some Japanese spoken.
Innkeepers: Wendy Hatfield and Ken Torbert.

*Garberville*

## Benbow Inn
445 Lake Benbow Drive
Garberville, California 95440
Telephone (707) 923-2124

"Since Chuck and Patsy Watts bought the inn about five years ago, many improvements have been made without sacrificing the original charm. The rooms have all been refurnished with king- and queen-size beds and new carpeting. Also, the upstairs hallways have new carpeting and cherrywood paneling.

"In the lobby and dining room there are several antique clocks, as well as a recently installed antique mantel over the fireplace in the lobby. A new fireplace has also been added in the cocktail lounge, and there is now a giant TV screen in the room off the lounge for showing old-time movies. The grounds are always colorful with beautiful English gardens.

"Yet another project has begun: the lengthy one of completely redoing the bathrooms."        —*David and Donna Mullin*

Open end of March to early December and for the Christmas season.
56 rooms, all with private bath.
Rates $58–$75, deluxe $95–$135, from $115 with fireplace.
Credit cards: American Express, MasterCard, Visa.
German spoken.
Greyhound bus service to Eureka.
Innkeepers: Chuck and Patsy Watts.

_____*Gualala*

**St. Orres**
36601 Highway 1
Gualala, California 95445
Telephone (707) 884-3303

"St. Orres takes one by surprise. You've driven two hours north of San Francisco on California coast Highway 1, totally enchanted by the bright sun sparkling off the surf of the Pacific Ocean, when a rise in the road drops away to present an irresistible Byzantine structure. This hotel was constructed by a group of five craftspeople with lumber from an old redwood trestle. There are onion domes and stained-glass windows. The building and the homey informality of the owners blend to make a unique environment unsurpassed for relaxation and good feelings.

"Upstairs are eight wood-paneled rooms with outside views of the ocean or surrounding forest. Here too there are individual touches, such as locally picked flowers and hand-sewn quilts. There are no television sets and telephones. Guests are offered a complimentary continental breakfast (and the anxious coffee drinker can always sneak in early through the back screen door). Weekend lunch and the daily dinner menu feature, in my opinion, some of the finest French cuisine of the West Coast. The *carré d'agneau persillé* (roast rack of lamb), coquilles St. Jacques (scallops in wine sauce), and bouillabaisse *marseillaise* (hearty fish soup), served with fine Napa Valley wine, are superb. Be sure to leave room for St. Orres's own embarrassingly satisfying dessert, Chocolate Decadence."

—*Wally Olsen*

Open all year, except January.
8 rooms with shared baths; 3 cottages, all with private bath.
Rates $50–$60 rooms, $60–$95 cottages, including continental breakfast.
Credit cards: MasterCard, Visa.
Transportation available to inn from Ocean Ridge airport, serving small planes.
Innkeepers: Charles T. Black and Rosemary Campiformio.

_____*Healdsburg*

**Grape Leaf Inn**
539 Johnson Street
Healdsburg, California 95448
Telephone (707) 433-8140

"The Grape Leaf Inn is a turn-of-the-century Victorian house located in a quiet residential area in the heart of the Sonoma County wine country. A large porch and adjoining parlor provide a restful setting for breakfast and frequently held wine tastings. Guests are served a full breakfast; the variety and individuality of the meal are a real pleasure. Mr. Terry Sweet, the innkeeper, and his staff are always available to assist their guests by recommending wineries to visit, restaurants in the area (menus available at the inn), and recreational activities on the nearby Russian River (swimming, float trips, picnics, canoeing, etc.). A specially recommended excursion would be to visit the wineries located in the beautiful Alexander Valley, which is only minutes from the Grape Leaf Inn. This area, and most of the Sonoma County Wine Country, is noted for its fine wines and has the additional advantage of being far less crowded with tourists than nearby Napa Valley. This plus the hospitality of the Grape Leaf Inn provides a wonderful opportunity for a relaxing and enjoyable time just an hour north of San Francisco."          —*R. J. Stockhus*

"We enjoyed a beautiful weekend in this charming bed-and-breakfast inn. It offered a country-town atmosphere with elegant accommodations. Our breakfast was delicious and very enjoyable, offering time to share with others the secrets and adventures of the wine country."          —*Mr. and Mrs. W. B. James*

"The inn is very nicely decorated, clean, and quiet, with a friendly innkeeper. Breakfast is like a gourmet meal in variety and presentation."          —*Deborah Norris*

Open all year.
4 rooms, all with private bath.
Rates from $45, including breakfast.
Credit cards: MasterCard, Visa.
Innkeeper: Tracy Logan Dickson.

_____*Inverness Park*

**Holly Tree Inn**
3 Silverhills Road
Inverness Park, California 94956
Telephone (415) 663-1554

Mailing Address:
Box 642
Point Reyes Station, California 94956

"The Holly Tree nestles in a beautifully wooded glen off Sir Francis Drake Boulevard. The rooms are simply but beautifully decorated, my favorite being the Laurel Room, all blue and white, airy and fresh, with a king-size bed. The three other rooms are done just as imaginatively, and descend in size. All, however, are extremely comfortable. When we were there, breakfast consisted of fresh strawberries and grapes, fresh-squeezed orange juice, a spinach-and-mushroom quiche, and both poppyseed and banana breads in addition to coffee, Sanka, or tea. The food is served in front of a fireplace in the dining room at a cozy little table. The opportunity to chat with innkeeper Diane Balough is as much a part of the joy of this place as the accommodations. The area abounds with wild flowers, birds, and trees. Mark it a small treasure."   —*Shelly Wile*

Open all year, except 2 weeks in January.
4 rooms, 2 with private bath.
Rates $50–$60, including full breakfast.
No credit cards.
Golden Gate Transit or Inverness buses to Point Reyes.
Innkeepers: Diane and Tom Balough.

---

*Julian*

## Julian Gold Rush Hotel
2032 Main Street (Box 856)
Julian, California 92036
Telephone (619) 765-0201

"My wife and I tried the Julian Gold Rush Hotel on a travel recommendation in our local newspaper. We found it to be everything it was said to be. The proprietors, Steve and Gig Ballinger, are gracious hosts. The hotel, which opened in 1887, still retains Victorian flavor with four-poster beds and facilities down the hall. Each room is named after a famous person of the time. (Ours was the Lloyd George Room.) We found the room and bath facilities clean and comfortable and, to our delight, we got a full hot breakfast with all the trimmings delivered to the room. There is also an adjoining honeymoon cottage with private bath."

—*Mr. and Mrs. Fred S. Clare*

Open all year.
15 rooms, including Honeymoon House, 3 with private bath.
Rates $21–$26 single, $38–$52 double with shared bath, $48–$58 double with private bath, $55–$70 Honeymoon House, including full breakfast.

No credit cards.
Innkeepers: Steve and Gig Ballinger.

_____*Laguna Beach*

**Eiler's Inn**
741 South Coast Highway
Laguna Beach, California 92651
Telephone (714) 494-3004

"Within the sound of the surf, Eiler's encircles a charming patio, where cheese and wine are served in the evenings. Once in the heart of Laguna's 'hippie hollow,' Eiler's has been effectively and charmingly renovated. A breakfast may include orange sections garnished with fresh mint snipped from the patio garden."

—*N. Kennedy*

Open all year.
11 rooms, 1 suite, all with private bath.
Rates $85–$95 rooms, suites $135, including breakfast and wine and cheese.
Credit cards: MasterCard, Visa.
Danish, French, and German spoken.
Limousine service to airport.
Innkeepers: Jonna Iversen, Kay Trepp, Annette and Henk Wirtz.

_____*La Jolla*

**La Valencia Hotel**
1132 Prospect
La Jolla, California 92037
Telephone (714) 454-0771

"To register at La Valencia is to enter a world of solid comfort and graceful pleasure. The staff combines cheerfully unobtrusive efficiency with old-fashioned courtesy. The place is beautiful in the Spanish style and immaculately maintained. My favorite place for lunch or dinner is the Whaling Bar and Grill. And the view of the Pacific Ocean from the other main dining room, the Sky Room, is a feast for the eye that quite matches the culinary feast. That is another thing about La Valencia: the food is never less than very good and more often it is superb. The kitchen and dining room staff always remember precisely what one has ordered, and the service maintains its dignity. The wine list is excellent and the prices sane.

La Valencia is not staffed by robots with their palms open for tips, but by wonderfully helpful professionals who know their jobs perfectly and appear to enjoy doing them.

"The swimming pool, with its Jacuzzi hot spring bath, is a splendid place to relax. But the point of being at La Valencia is that it is the best hotel of any I know in which to have a relaxing and civilized time. It is a haven of the good life. La Valencia is a rare blend of dignity and authentic hospitality, without a trace of folksy backslapping or phony friendliness. Rather, La Valencia deserves a national award as one of the most civilized places in the United States. Yet there is not the slightest stuffiness about it, and it is on no nostalgia trip. La Valencia is the real thing in the real world, which only proves that the good and graceful things of life are still amply available somewhere—if you know where to go."
—*Professor Philip Rieff; also recommended by Louisa L. Becker*

Open all year.
100 rooms, all with private bath.
Rates $75–$95 single, $10 extra for second person.
Credit cards: American Express, MasterCard, Visa.
French and Spanish spoken.
Air and rail service to San Diego, 23 miles away.
Manager: Richard P. Irwin.

## *Los Alamos*

**1880 Union Hotel**
362 Bell Street
Los Alamos, California 93440
Telephone: Ask operator for area code 805, Los Alamos 2744

"Los Alamos (California, not New Mexico) on U.S. 101 is a town not a bit larger now than in the 1880s when its hotel opened. Owner Dick Langdon, an enterprising Los Angeles emigré, and Jim Radhe, his architect in residence, have recreated another era: Victorian, Western, perfect. There is a salon, a dining hall and, beyond the swinging doors, the bar where Langdon sometimes plays the upright piano. The furnishings, being suitably 'crowded,' are right for the period. Dinner and drinks are sturdy and oddly wholesome, perhaps because their recipes date from the 1800s. After dinner there's no TV, no phones. Instead, there is brandy, sinfully fresh fruit popovers, and shooting pool in the upstairs salon. There is even a well-stocked library. A great part of the charm of the place is chatting with other guests. In the bedrooms you find waiting a carafe of wine and two glasses. Some of the rooms share a bath. And, are you ready for this? The bathtub is sheet copper, authentically postbellum.

"Langdon, consistent in his quest for a total period experience, now has a 1918 white touring car for motoring in the beautiful surrounding countryside. Breakfast is served punctually and family style. Check the time and don't be late. On each table a bottle of brandy sits next to the coffeepot. Like everything else, just the way it was in the old West."   —*Richard and Wendy Kahlenberg*

Open Fridays, Saturdays, and Sundays all year.
14 rooms, 4 with private bath.
Rates $65–$90, including breakfast.
No credit cards.
Innkeepers: Dick, Teri, Marianne, and Marijane Langdon.

## *Los Olivos*

**Red Rooster Ranch**
2681 Oakcrest Lane (Box 554)
Los Olivos, California 93441
Telephone (805) 688-8050

"Finding this extraordinary bed-and-breakfast ranch was like discovering a part of one's soul that needed completion. The ranch guesthouse and main home are situated in the magnificent meadows of the Santa Ynez Valley, surrounded by majestic mountains, horse farms, and wineries. The rooms are immaculate, charming, and beautiful, each unique with warmth, comfort, and serenity. The owners are fabulously warm and educated people who generously open their home to excellent conversation, incredibly good American and country French food and wine, and a warm fireplace on a chilly evening, providing a sense of new friendship that is incomparable. This is a rare treasure and a fabulous find for the traveler who insists on quality and comfort."   —*David B. Kaminsky*

Open all year.
7 rooms, 5 with private bath; 1 suite with kitchen.
Rates $65–$75, suite $120, including breakfast.
No credit cards.
Innkeepers: Casey and Connell Cowan.

Turn to the back of this book for pages inviting *your* comments

## _Mendocino_

## MacCallum House
45020 Albion Street (Box 206)
Mendocino, California 95460
Telephone (707) 937-0289

"MacCallum House was a wedding gift to Daisy Kelley from her father in 1882. Today, it is indeed a delightful gift to the traveler. This historic Victorian inn, situated near the rugged coast of northern California, has an enviable view of the Pacific Ocean. Enter the white picket gate and ascend the stairs to a welcoming entrance. In the foyer one is introduced to the Kelley-MacCallum family: mounted on the side wall is a glass case of photographs and a résumé of the heritage of the house. Choosing a room, whether in the main house or separate cottages, is not easy, unless one is set on an ocean view. Each room has its unique charm and warmth, and all are impeccably clean. Armoires, bedsteads, Tiffany lamps, and tables are enhanced by well-chosen wallpaper, homespun bedspreads, and batiste curtains. The upstairs sitting room affords relaxed reading. Here are interesting literature, historical papers, and the _pièce de résistance:_ several volumes of Daisy Kelley MacCallum's fascinating and informative scrapbook. The day is complete with dinner in the residence dining room (a favorite: freshly caught salmon), followed by a visit to the Gray Whale Bar in the glassed-in porch overlooking the ocean."                 —_Helen M. Menken_

"MacCallum House was beyond reproach, with one exception: from my room on the second floor I could distinctly hear music from the bar after I had retired for the night. The furnishings, the surroundings, the weather, the food, the service, the atmosphere were, other than that, so perfect that I really did not mind. The MacCallum House met all my hopes and far exceeded my expectations. I highly recommend that anyone visiting Mendocino walk as long as possible along the desolate seacoast, return to MacCallum House for a shower, and have dinner as late as possible. It would be a shame to waste the magnificent view and the invigorating air."
                                                      —_Phyllis Faber Kelley_

Open all year.
20 rooms, 2 suites, 5 with private bath.
Rates $35–$100, including continental breakfast.
Credit cards: MasterCard, Visa.
Spanish spoken.
Innkeeper: Jess Swain.

## Mendocino Hotel
45080 Main Street (Box 587)
Mendocino, California 95460
Telephone (707) 937-0511

"Mendocino, situated on bluffs high above the Pacific, north of San Francisco, is a village founded about the time of the California gold rush. It has been declared a historic monument. The architecture is Victorian and American Gothic, with many patterns of shingle, weathered or in crisp white, blue, and yellow. Many of the houses or cottages are shops or galleries of fine quality. The atmosphere of creativity is an inspiration to artists, writers, and those of us who enjoy their works. Then there is the magnificent sea, smashing waves and huge rock formations, wonderful for fishermen, naturalists, and photographers. Nearby are the awesome redwood forests and the famous Skunk steam trains that take one on the old logging route over trestles and through tunnels.

"Coming home to the hotel is another joy. It faces the bay and is comfortably 'done' in the best Victorian tradition. The parlor or lounge will have a fine fire to gather around, and perhaps a chess game going on in a corner. The bar is attractive—in the Art Nouveau motif of the late nineteenth century. The bedrooms have canopied brass beds, with wallpaper and draperies in softly patterned colors to match. If the nights are cool, Oscar the pigeon might come in through the window to roost on top of the wardrobe until morning. He is friendly, elusive, and determined."    —*Dorothy Burgert*

Open all year.
24 rooms, 2 suites, 12 with private bath.
Rates $45–$70 with shared bath, $65–$140 with private bath, including continental breakfast.
Credit cards: American Express, MasterCard, Visa.
Manager: R. O. Peterson.

# *Mokelumne Hill*

## Hotel Léger
Main and Leffert Streets
Mokelumne Hill, California 95245
Telephone (209) 286-1401

"The Mother Lode Country, as the vicinity of Highway 49 is called, is one of the few areas of California where asparagus ferns do not sprout in the windows of trendy cafés and where historical artifacts have been allowed to molder gracefully. One can drive for days checking up on towns with names like Angel's Camp and Volcano, where things have never been the same since the gold rush days of the mid-nineteenth century. Each town bears its version of the International Order of Odd Fellows hall, a post office/general store, and a hotel.

"The Hotel Léger offers a pleasing combination of historic authenticity and modern convenience. The hotel bar features Victorian decor and rowdy humor, while the restaurant serves up unusually delicious prime ribs. Guests can linger after dinner on the long porch of the building fronting the main street or take a refreshing dip in the pool concealed in the leafy backyard. The owners are proud to show off the old wine cellar, the vaudeville theater next door, and the historic objects found around the property. All in all, a delightful stopover for the wistful prospector."

—*Jean Carlton Parker*

Open all year.
11 rooms, 2 suites, 7 with private bath.
Rates $27 shared bath, $40 private bath, $46 suites.
No credit cards.
Private airstrip at St. Andress, 7 miles away.
Innkeeper: Brandy Clark.

## _____ *Monterey*

**The Jabberwock**
598 Laine Street
Monterey, California 93940
Telephone (408) 372-4777

"The Jabberwock, after the creature in Lewis Carroll's poem "Jabberwocky" from *Through the Looking-Glass,* is a large, remodeled Victorian home that once was a nunnery. It is set on a half-acre of sculptured gardens and waterfalls just four blocks from Cannery Row. The antique furniture and many special appointments and decorative touches are charming. Innkeepers Barbara and Jim Allen have created a special atmosphere for people to meet, relax, and enjoy each other. For example, Sherry Hour at 5 P.M. is a social occasion. We met a *very* nice couple from Los Angeles while enjoying the sherry and excellent hors d'oeuvres and had dinner with them at the restaurant recommended by Barbara. Breakfast, too, was a wonderful social occasion. All five couples staying at the inn that weekend lingered for two and a half hours over Barbara's breakfast feast called Razzleberry Flabjas. Breakfast the next day was Humpty Dumpty—juice, fresh fruit, croissants, cheeses, and other goodies.

"Our room, the Borogrove (once again from the poem) was a large suite with sitting area, king-size bed with down comforter, private bath, and expansive view of the Monterey Bay. The other four rooms also have special "Jabberwocky" names—Mome Raths, the Toves, Tulgey Wood, and the Brillig—with distinctive decorations suggestive of their names."                    —*Rand Heer*

Open all year.
5 rooms, 2 with private bath.
Rates $75–$115, including breakfast.
No credit cards.
French, Danish, and Spanish spoken.
Innkeepers: Jim and Barbara Allen.

---

**Old Monterey Inn**
500 Martin Street
Monterey, California 93940
Telephone (408) 375-8284

"In our travels from Hawaii to Europe there is one inn brighter than all the others—the Old Monterey Inn. Judy and I have stayed there a number of times, and if it hadn't been a matter of first having to get someone to look after our six children, it would have been a great number of times. The inn itself is one of the finest old homes I've ever seen, in a great setting."                    —*Jim Ryan*

"My wife and I are aficionados of inns. Our stay at the Old Monterey Inn was without flaw and cannot be equaled by any other establishment we have visited. We highly recommend this inn."
                    —*P. Totman*

Open all year.
10 rooms, 8 with private bath.
Rates $95–$160, including continental breakfast and wine and cheese.
No credit cards.

Airport limousine service.
Innkeepers: Ann and Gene Swett.

_____*Murphys*

**Dunbar House 1880**
271 Jones Street (Box 1375)
Murphys, California 95247
Telephone (209) 728-2897

"Dunbar House is a brand-new bed-and-breakfast in a very historic (for California) area. We enjoyed the hospitality, room, and breakfast—all nicely handled. We highly recommend it to anyone seeking a place reminiscent of gold rush days."   —*Robert H. Knollin*

Open all year.
5 rooms with shared baths.
Rates $45–$55, including breakfast.
No credit cards.
Portuguese spoken.
Innkeepers: John and Barbara Carr.

_____*Napa*

**The Beazley House**
1910 First Street
Napa, California 94558
Telephone (707) 257-1649

"The structure itself dates back to the early 1900s, and the present owners are maintaining its early appeal and authenticity. The house is warm and cozy, with beautiful stained-glass windows and doors. Antique furniture is functionally and tastefully arranged throughout the house, while colorful handmade quilts adorn the brass beds.

"Located in the heart of downtown Napa, it is within walking distance of shops and restaurants. It is also a ten-minute drive to the valley's wineries. The Beazleys are terrific hosts and have a great deal of pride in and enthusiasm for their home. Three generations live and work there together."   —*John Brodeur*

"Located in a very well preserved Victorian era neighborhood, the main house, carriage building, and grounds occupy half a large block. There are plans to remodel the carriage house for guests, but for now there are half a dozen rooms, each with its own distinctive antique furniture and hand-sewn bedspreads. The sun room, for instance, has its own balcony and overlooks the grounds and surrounding mansions. The master bedroom is very large and has its own fireplace. All the appointments of an early Victorian home can be found here: beautiful antiques, curved landing with window seat, and ornamental woodwork.

"I don't know if Carol Beazley's muffin recipes are a secret or not, but the bran muffins I had on my first visit and the banana muffins I tried on my second were unlike anything I've ever tasted. They also set out large platters of fresh fruit, and serve tea, coffee, and fruit juices. Gets you off to a good start for touring wineries, museums, or the nearby hot springs."                      —*Fred Hinners*

Open all year.
8 rooms, 4 with private bath, 2 with private hot tub.
Rates $65–$85, including continental breakfast.
Credit cards: MasterCard, Visa.
Innkeepers: Jim, Carol, Sonja, Scott, J. C., and Marilee Beazley.

_____*Nevada City*

**National Hotel**
211 Broad Street
Nevada City, California 95959
Telephone (916) 265-4551

"Reputed to be the oldest hostelry in continuous operation in California, the venerable and historic National Hotel of picturesque Nevada City first opened its doors to the public in 1854. Today, it combines authentic Victorian gold rush atmosphere with modern comforts, pool, and a popular cuisine. The bar is the social hub of town. The National is surrounded by numerous shops and fine restaurants, catering to local as well as tourist trade. Gas streetlights, stately homes, and ornate sidewalk porticoes add their embellishments to a once-fabled mining town anchored peacefully amid the tall pines along the banks of Deer Creek. The hotel, museums, and shops operate year round, with visitors returning often to enjoy the distinct seasons and holiday decor of this important heritage center, located on a scenic highway between Sacramento and Lake Tahoe. Because of the many cultural events held at the historic Nevada Theatre—Mark Twain once lectured there—it is advisable to make reservations at the National, particularly on weekends."                      —*James W. Lenhoff*

Open all year.
43 rooms, 30 with private bath.

Rates $26–$57.
Credit cards: American Express, MasterCard, Visa.
Greyhound bus service.
Innkeeper: Tom Coleman.

_____ *Ojai*

## Ojai Valley Inn and Country Club
Country Club Drive (P.O. Box L)
Ojai, California 93023
Telephone (805) 646-5511

Most establishments with more than 100 guest rooms should very
likely be called hotels. Not the Ojai Valley Inn and Country Club.
The charm of the inn has not been the least bit diluted over the
years by room additions. Where else can you sit right in the middle
of the lobby and play checkers? (It had been so long since we had
played that we had to ask for instructions.) You can eat your meals
in the dining room overlooking the beautiful Ojai Valley (and it is
beautiful), or dine on the back patio overlooking the championship
golf course (one of the inn's big attractions). There's also swimming, horseback riding, and tennis (all on the premises). The inn
is just over an hour's drive from Los Angeles and offers a wonderful
place to get away for a week or a weekend. For years, celebrities have
used the inn as a private getaway. Sports jackets are required for
men in the restaurant at night.          —*Robert Newman*

Open all year.
107 rooms, all with private bath.
Rates $120–$160 single, $140–$185 double; AP.
No credit cards.
Managing director: William Briggs.

_____ *Pacific Grove*

## Centrella Hotel
612 Central Avenue
Pacific Grove, California 93950
Telephone (408) 372-3372

"The Centrella Hotel is a newly refurbished bed-and-breakfast inn
near Cannery Row and the ocean. It is filled with antiques, reproductions, Laura Ashley designs, and imported English textiles. The
cottages have individual fireplaces. Dr. Megna and Jeanne Dreyer,
manager and innkeeper, host a get-together each evening for guests

with a light repast of pâtés, cheeses, biscuits, bread, fresh vegetables with dips, and a lovely sherry. Breakfast consists of juices, cereal, sweet rolls, coffee or tea. It is delightful. Proof: one couple stayed 40 days and 40 nights."         —*Dr. and Mrs. A. P. Cullen*

"The old Victorian mansion has been tastefully converted with individually decorated rooms and cottages. The long row of French windows overlooks a lovely little garden and captures all the morning sunlight. The Centrella is one of the most delightful bed-and-breakfast hotels I've visited."         —*Barbara R. Adams*

"This all new Victorian Hotel, circa 1890, is a most charming place. It rained the whole weekend so we spent a lot of time in the parlor with great breakfasts and sherry and snacks at the 5:30 get-together. Everybody had a grand time. We recommend it to anyone going to the Carmel–Big Sur–Pebble Beach–Monterey area."

—*John B. Spear*

"What an absolutely fantastic experience! Remember the delightful feeling you get when you are a guest for dinner or the weekend, and your hostess has obviously thought of you as someone special? At the Centrella, you're subtly aware that in the eyes of the innkeeper you are a VIP. Everything is done for your pleasure, yet in a most unobtrusive fashion."         —*Janice K. Barden*

Open all year.
20 rooms, 2 suites, 5 cottages, 16 with private bath.
Rates $50–$65 shared bath, $75–$95 private bath, $100–$125 suites, $120–$150 cottages, including continental breakfast and evening hors d'oeuvres and sherry.
Credit cards: American Express, MasterCard, Visa.
Italian spoken.
Innkeeper: Jeanne Dreyer.

---

## The Gosby House Inn
643 Lighthouse Avenue
Pacific Grove, California 93950
Telephone (408) 375-1287

"A restored Victorian mansion, full of leaded glass, brass, and wood. There is an antique doll collection displayed in the entry parlor. Nearby is Cannery Row, made famous by John Steinbeck; Carmel-by-the-Sea; and the coastline of Big Sur. Breakfast, which comes with the room charge, is served in the common room. The inn is right on Lighthouse Avenue, about two blocks from the bay-front. The rooms are attractive and clean."

—*Mrs. Bartley M. Harloe*

Open all year.
19 rooms, 13 with private bath.
Rates $50–$75, including continental breakfast. No smoking.
No credit cards.
Inn has antique taxi for meeting guests at Monterey airport. Grey-hound buses (which meet trains at Salinas) drop visitors close to inn.
Managers: Ralph and Kit Sotzing.

# Piercy

**Hartsook Inn**
Piercy, California 95467
Telephone (707) 247-3305

"The inn is actually a collection of rustic cottages hidden away in a thirty-acre grove of redwoods on both sides of U.S. Highway 101. One lodge contains a gift shop, lobby, and dining room, serving simple but excellent fresh fare. The location on the banks of the Eel River affords bathing and fishing; the river's gentle current will carry you slowly downstream, and you can hike back up for another ride. Trails from the inn lead hikers off into the redwoods—to Richardson Grove, to the Hartsook Giant (59 feet in circumfer-ence), to a lookout point above the Eel River. Some cabins have kitchens; others are only bedrooms and baths."

—*Margaret Zeigler*

Open April 15 to November 1.
62 rooms, all with private bath.
Rates $28–$40, housekeeping units $40–$46.
Credit cards: MasterCard, Visa.
Piercy is a Greyhound bus flag stop.
Innkeeper: Julie Willows.

# Rancho Santa Fe

**The Inn at Rancho Santa Fe**
Linca del Circle at Pasco Delicias (Box 869)
Rancho Santa Fe, California 92067
Telephone (619) 756-1131

The Rancho Santa Fe area was little more than a barren waste when, in 1845, the last Mexican governor of California granted almost 9,000 acres of it to Juan Osuna, a Spanish soldier of fortune who had become alcalde of the Pueblo of San Diego. In 1906 the Santa Fe Railroad bought the grant from Osuna's heirs and named it Rancho Santa Fe. The railroad had an ambitious plan: the area would be planted with eucalyptus trees that in time would grow into an endless supply of railway ties. Unfortunately, the wood turned out to be unsuitable for the purpose, and the railroad was left with lush scenery but useless land.

"The inn is located in the center of an old-fashioned village mostly inhabited by the very rich of good breeding (not the nouveaux riches, although some have infiltrated). It resembles some of the old-fashioned inns I have visited in New England, and the setting is beautiful. The cottages are well appointed, comfortable, and meticulously clean.

"Most of the guests at the inn seem to be in the senior citizen class of higher means—many are Easterners in search of clement skies or aficionados of horse racing during the Del Mar season (July to mid-September)."                                   —*Louisa L. Becker*

"There were many golfers in the over-fifty-five bracket. It is popular with officers from the naval station nearby; my husband was addressed as 'Commander' by another guest—he looks pretty authoritative with his silver sideburns. The grounds are handsomely landscaped. There are more restaurants in the area now."
                                                      —*Camille J. Cook*

Open all year.
80 rooms, all with private bath.
Rates $45–$95, cottages and suites from $150.
Credit cards: American Express, MasterCard, Visa.
French, German, and Spanish spoken.
No public transportation in area. Cars can be rented at San Diego or La Jolla.
Innkeeper: Dan Royce.

———————————————————————*Reedley*

**Hotel Burgess**
1726 11th Street
Reedley, California 93654
Telephone (209) 638-6315

"I was in Reedley on business, the hotel's sign outside of town caught my eye, and I found the Burgess a delightful place. It has been completely restored and the rooms are done with a variety of international themes such as the San Francisco room, the Polynesian room, the Indian room, the Brazilian room, the Austrian room, the French room, the Moroccan room, the Oriental room, and the U.S. Today room."                    —*Joseph L. Neal*

Open all year.
18 rooms, all with private bath.
Rates $24–$60.
Credit cards: MasterCard, Visa.
Greyhound bus service from Fresno twice daily. Municipal airport in Reedley.
Manager: Michele Corcoran.

_____*Sacramento*

## Amber House
1315 22nd Street
Sacramento, California 95816
Telephone (916) 444-8085

"Built in 1907, Amber House is in one of Sacramento's old residential neighborhoods just seven blocks from the State Capitol and downtown shopping.

"The house has been restored with great care—from the living room's antique glass doors to the boxed beam ceilings. I liked the added amenities, too: a complimentary bottle of wine in the guest rooms and California sherry in the library (a room guests can use for small meetings). The bedrooms are furnished with antiques; one seventy-year-old porcelain tub is extraordinary, but it would take me some time to get used to the skylight and trees overhead.

"Breakfast is served in your room on Limoges china. Innkeeper Robert O'Neil bakes his own pastry and blends the house coffee, both of which are delicious."                    —*Eileen Boland*

Open all year.
4 rooms, 2 with private bath.
Rates $65–$75, including breakfast.
Credit cards: American Express, MasterCard, Visa.
Innkeepers: William McOmber and Robert O'Neil.


If you would like to amend, update, or disagree with any entry, write now.

**The Briggs House**
2209 Capitol Avenue
Sacramento, California 95816
Telephone (916) 441-3214

"The front porch of the Briggs House is so spacious that the cord
of firewood stacked opposite the porch swing looks inconspicuous.
The house was built in 1901 and restored in 1980–81 to its proper
grandeur. The common rooms and bedrooms are decorated with
period furniture and antiques. Modern hotels can't compete with
this kind of spaciousness and comfort.

"Each guest receives a basket of treats upon arrival. Breakfast,
served in a common area, consists of homemade bread, fresh fruit
or juice, and coffee and tea. Bikes are available for touring Sacramento—Capitol Park, Sutter's Fort and the Indian Museum, the
Convention Center, and the newly restored Capitol itself are only
blocks away." *—Beverly Nelson*

Open all year.
6 rooms, 3 with private bath.
Rates $45–$90, including breakfast.
Credit cards: American Express, MasterCard, Visa.
Innkeepers: Bob and Sue Garmston, Barbara Stoltz, Kathy Yeates,
   Paula Rawles, Donna Bowman, Mary Cramer.

## St. Helena

**Hotel St. Helena**
1309 Main Street
St. Helena, California 94574
Telephone (707) 963-4388

"The St. Helena is a charming little turn-of-the-century bed-and-
breakfast hotel. Recently restored and redecorated, it offers delightful accommodations at a reasonable price. Breakfast is a family affair
with cold orange juice, homemade muffins, and coffee. Weary from
a day of winery sightseeing, guests are offered wine as they sit in the
downstairs parlor. This hotel is truly a must if you are tired of sterile
chain hotels and motels at high prices." *—R. A. Beaudette*

"Absolutely first class. The service is very personal and attentive.
The housekeeping is immaculate and the decor beautiful as well as
functional. The public rooms are very comfy." *—Adrian Affrunti*

"It's a fun hotel and a change from the high-rises. As it is 100 years old, you get a feeling of how things must have been years ago."
—*Kay Griffin*

"The rooms are exquisite—all done in antiques with high beds and freestanding bathtubs. What a romantic spot, with little touches like fresh flowers and fruit."                              —*Diane Umstead*

"Absolutely charming!"                          —*Mr. and Mrs. Joe Petrone*

Open all year.
17 rooms, 1 suite, 14 with private bath.
Rates $50 shared bath, $65–$80 private bath, $95 suite, including
    continental breakfast.
Credit cards: MasterCard, Visa.
Innkeeper: Ralph Usina.

---

## The Wine Country Inn
1152 Lodi Lane
St. Helena, California 94574
Telephone (707) 936-7077

"The towels are so deliciously thick at the Smith family's Wine Country Inn that you can't dry inside your ears. Each room is artfully and individually decorated in country style. Some are accented with framed examples of Grandma Smith's stitchery, and others have weathered barn siding as paneling. Some of the rooms have fireplaces with kindling properly laid on days cool enough for a fire. Other rooms have the comfort of private terraces or balconies. Only breakfast is included here—warm baked goods and California juice and fruit in season. It is served in the entry-level common room, and it gives the opportunity for meeting fellow guests to compare notes on the sights, restaurants, winery tours, and tasting rooms of the Napa Valley. One of the family (most often son Jim) will be on hand to offer tourist advice while he refills your coffee cup.

"The building (new in 1975, with an addition completed in 1979) sits tall on a treeless plot adjacent to a sixty-year-old olive grove in the center of the Napa Valley. The inn is off Route 29/128, which is studded with tasting rooms that give away glasses of vin ordinaire and sell finer bottlings.

"There is minimal tourist interest outside the wineries. The town of Sonoma has restored some buildings pertaining to early California history that may be visited en route from San Francisco."
—*Camille J. Cook*

"We recently visited the Wine Country Inn and concur with your recommendation."                    —*Elnora Robinson*

"We loved every single minute spent in this lovely inn. The rooms were spacious and homey, the family and staff friendly. The tranquil setting was gorgeous. We will go back."          —*Carla Sanders*

"At the Wine Country Inn in St. Helena, we had a pleasant, large room with a small patio. The breakfasts were all they were cracked up to be. At $90, though, we thought it a bit expensive."
                                                            —*Hilary Rubinstein*

Open all year, except 2 weeks just prior to Christmas.
25 rooms, all with private bath.
Rates $78–$110, including breakfast.
Credit cards: MasterCard, Visa.
¼ mile from Greyhound bus stop (Lodi Lane and Highway 29/128).
Innkeeper: Jim Smith.

---

# San Diego

## Britt House
406 Maple Street
San Diego, California 92103
Telephone (619) 234-2926

"I have been enthusiastically recommending this old converted family home to friends visiting San Diego. Each room has a special decor. The innkeeper served me breakfast in my room, which I ate by a window overlooking the garden. I also had afternoon tea and then found cookies and fruit in my room in the evening. I want to go back."                                —*Camilla Tanner*

Open all year.
9 rooms, 1 with private bath.
Rates $63–$95, including breakfast and afternoon tea, sauna.
Credit Cards: MasterCard, Visa.
French spoken.
Innkeeper: Daun Martin.

Do you know a hotel in your state that we have overlooked? Write *now*.

*San Francisco*

## Bed and Breakfast Inn
4 Charlton Court
San Francisco, California 94123
Telephone (415) 921-9784

This inn was created by Robert and Marily Kavanaugh in a pre-earthquake Victorian mansion in a quiet corner off Union Street with its shops and restaurants. Rooms here are all endowed with their own personalities. Most interesting is a penthouse flat with a spiral staircase leading to a bedroom loft. Marily says it is a favorite for anniversaries and honeymoons and such. In all rooms, guests get breakfast in bed.

"The Bed and Breakfast Inn tops my list of favorite places to spend a night or weekend. This inn is charming, delightful, alluring, and lovely. Reservations are a must." —*Rich Wiesner*

"The Mayfair, the penthouse apartment at the Bed and Breakfast Inn, is everything the most exacting traveler could ask for. It is a beautiful setting for a romantic evening or a comfortable rendez-vous for friends from afar. In fact, it is hard to leave the place even to see all that San Francisco has to offer!
"The other rooms, however, are small, though charming, and not all have space for breakfast in bed. The location on Union Street is delightful; one can wander about the shops, clubs and restaurants."
—*Sandy and Geoff Lamb*

Open all year.
9 rooms and suites, 5 with private bath.
Rates $48–$72 shared bath, $80–$158 private bath, $158 penthouse
    flat. Breakfast included.
No credit cards.
French, German, Italian, and Spanish spoken.
Innkeepers: Robert and Marily Kavanaugh.

## El Cortez Hotel
550 Geary Street
San Francisco, California 94102
Telephone (415) 775-5000

"If you are looking for a reasonably priced, pleasant hotel within easy reach of Union Square, you can't do better than the El Cortez. Architecturally, it is an amazing mixture of Mexican and twenties American. Once in our room, we discovered comfortable beds, a clean bright bathroom, a dressing room, and a small but well-equipped kitchen. The last is a boon, saving the money one usually spends in hotels on room service. The hotel has a restaurant, which looked promising, but when we weren't cooking for ourselves, we explored the vast range of ethnic restaurants around town. We certainly prefer to stay at the El Cortez than at any of the ritzier and more expensive hotels in the center of San Francisco."

—*Maggie and Andrew de Lory*

Open all year.
175 rooms, all with private bath, most with kitchenettes.
Rates $38–$42 single, $44–$48 double, $60–$70 quadruple, $92–$150 suites.
Credit cards: American Express, Carte Blanche, Diners Club, MasterCard, Visa.
Spanish spoken.
Manager: Mel Osorio.

---

**Four Seasons–Clift Hotel**
495 Geary at Taylor Street
San Francisco, California 94102
Telephone (415) 775-4700

"With 402 rooms and suites, this hotel can hardly call itself 'little.' But this is San Francisco, after all, city of the Mark Hopkins, the St. Francis, the Fairmont, and what must surely be the most soaring Hyatt of them all. Next to them, the Clift is a country inn. And little is as little does. The Clift feels small enough that *Fortune* magazine, in October 1974, called it one of the world's eight great little-known hotels; that must be some measure of size.

"The Clift does things in a small way. There's a proper concierge, a morning paper with the room service breakfast (alongside weight-less croissants and tiny pots of Scottish marmalade and jam), free shoeshines, and a small brochure in each room outlining a walking tour of the neighborhood. The city has always felt a bit self-satisfied to us. But any place that's been called the most beautiful in America by Alistair Cooke, Georges Pompidou, and Nikita Khrushchev can be forgiven that."   —*Mechtild Hoppenrath and Charles Oberdorf*

"The Clift—as it is known to cognoscenti—is immediately contiguous to San Francisco's major legitimate theaters, department stores, specialty shops, ladies' and gentlemen's clubs, and some of the city's most distinguished restaurants. One of the last of such is the Redwood and another the French Room within the Clift, the first celebrating its glory in Art Deco designs in laminated wood, heightened by four major paintings by Gustav Klimt, and the second the *bon ton* one associates with the very best of France's five-star hotels. The latter is undoubtedly the West's most beautifully proportioned and decorated dining room in the grand manner.

"The Clift is small enough for singularly good service, yet large enough for the attention its clientele would expect of a human-scaled grand hotel. Mr. Allport, its stellar concierge of more than thirty years, is exceptional. Likewise, Greta, the housekeeper—also a San Francisco institution—will execute nearly any of the guests' wishes. The Clift has its own French laundry, which is amazingly fast and good."
                                                        —*Dr. F. M. Hinkhouse*

Open all year.
402 rooms, all with private bath.
Rates $140–$160 single, $134–$180 double.
Credit cards: Air Canada, American Express, Carte Blanche, Diners
    Club, MasterCard, Visa.
Many languages spoken.
Manager: Stan Bromley.

---

## Mansion Hotel
2220 Sacramento Street
San Francisco, California 94115
Telephone (415) 929-9444

In a neighborhood of some of San Francisco's finest old homes, the Mansion Hotel offers a bit of Victorian life, complete with parlor concerts of Bach and Mozart, a billiards room, and a sculpture garden. Rooms are all interesting, with those touches that made Victorian buildings so much fun: sloping ceilings, rounded bases, rich wood ornamentation. Though the neighborhood is residential, city buses connect the Mansion House with downtown San Francisco, Union Square, Fisherman's Wharf, and Ghirardelli Square. The cable car stop is four blocks away.

"When given my choice I pass on the Hiltons, Sheratons, and Hyatts and reserve at the Mansion for the opportunity of spending some special moments in another century. It's a hotel not just for travelers, for San Franciscans are often guests there. As the brochure points out, once you have entered the grand foyer you know you have arrived in another place, another time."     —*Rich Wiesner*

Open all year.
19 rooms, all with private bath.
Rates $64–$114 single, $79–$129 double, including breakfast in bed.
Credit cards: American Express, Diners Club, Carte Blanche, MasterCard, Visa.
French and Spanish spoken.
Can be reached by bus, taxi, or cable car.
Innkeeper: Charles Brown.

---

**The Obrero Hotel**
1208 Stockton
San Francisco, California 94133
Telephone (415) 986-9850

"The Obrero Hotel seems to delight foreign visitors. It is lazy, comfortable, unpretentious, and good value. Its rooms are adequate and the Basque food is abundant. Wine is served with each repast. Breakfast comes with the room and the coffee is good and strong. The clientele is fascinating. Basques from everywhere—Australia, South Africa, New Zealand, the Argentine, and Chile—seem to gather here and yarn each other with their exploits. The innkeeper, however, is from the Old Sod of Ireland and has a lilting accent. The staff is largely Cantonese, for you are in the heart of Chinatown."     —*Dr. F. M. Hinkhouse*

Open all year.
12 rooms with shared baths.
Rates $25–$45, including full European breakfast of meat, cheese, and eggs.
No credit cards.
Chinese, French, German, and Italian spoken.
Manager: Bambi MacDonald.

Rates quoted were the latest available. But they may not reflect unexpected increases or local and state taxes. Be sure to verify when you book.

## The Raphael
386 Geary Street
San Francisco, California 94102
Telephone (415) 986-2000

"A marvelous centrally located hotel with European overtones, it is a short distance from shops, theaters, and restaurants. The rooms are very well furnished and have two telephones each. If the Raphael is full, which it often is, the staff will help you find another hotel."                    —*Harry Kennedy, Jr.*

Open all year.
150 rooms, all with private bath.
Rates $63–$80 single, $75–$92 double.
Credit cards: American Express, Carte Blanche, Diners Club, MasterCard, Visa.
Chinese, French, German, Hungarian, Italian, Korean, and Spanish spoken.
Manager: Philip Creamer.

## Union Street Inn
2229 Union Street
San Francisco, California 94123
Telephone (415) 346-0424

Helen Stewart was a teacher who got laid off in a school cutback and decided to begin a new career as innkeeper in a large Edwardian house in San Francisco. Denise Perrier, a singer with an international background, assists in the running of the inn, which draws guests from home and abroad.

"What a treat this inn is as a retreat from city bustle, yet it is located in a lively area for eating and shopping. More important than its location and the beautifully decorated rooms is the warm welcome we received from Helen Stewart and her staff. There was hot coffee on a chilly, damp day as well as generous advice on places to eat and on transportation. It feels more like visiting with friends."
                    —*Neysa Ojalvo*

"Each room is so distinctly beautiful. What a marvelous break from the cold and impersonal hotels."                    —*Andrea Eisner*

Open all year.
5 rooms and a carriage house, 3 with private bath.
Rates: rooms $75–$114, carriage house $145, including breakfast.
Credit cards: American Express, MasterCard, Visa.
Spanish spoken.
Innkeepers: Helen Stewart and Jim Kiley.

---

## The Washington Square Inn
1660 Stockton Street
San Francisco, California 94133
Telephone (415) 981-4220

"Washington Square Inn is situated at the foot of Telegraph Hill—
the very heart of San Francisco. Despite its proximity to the financial
center of the West, the best of the city's restaurants, its stores,
shops, and theaters—and a blessedly short ride to the opera, the
symphony orchestra, and the museums—it is graced with quiet,
low-keyed elegance. The charm is reflected in its superbly appointed rooms, which feature, alternately, English and French antiques. The inn is kitty-corner from the Venetian Gothic Revival
Church of Saints Peter and Paul and from Mama's Restaurant. Thus
soul and body, body and soul are well served. For the delectation
of the inn's guests, breakfast is served in the rooms on Staffordshire,
or at an aging oak table situated directly in front of a roaring fire.
The concierge can arrange theater, opera, or concert tickets, a private secretary, a special tour—perhaps to Muir Woods or to Pebble
Beach—or nearly anything else one might need or want."
                                                —Dr. F. M. Hinkhouse

Open all year.
15 rooms, 11 with private bath.
Rates $60–$125 single, $70–$135 double, including continental
    breakfast and afternoon tea.
Credit cards: American Express, MasterCard, Visa.
Innkeepers: Norman and Nan Rosenblatt.

# San Luis Obispo

## The Madonna Inn
100 Madonna Road
San Luis Obispo, California 93401
Telephone (805) 543-3000

"San Simeon, William Randolph Hearst's castle, is just a few miles north, but we prefer Alex Madonna's monument to himself. Hearst had pretensions to taste; Madonna had no pretensions at all. Where to begin to describe this outrageous hotel? How about in the men's washroom of the coffee shop: The sinks are copper, set into a copper counter. The mirrors are copper paella pans with mirrored bottoms; the urinal, a solid copper trough flushed by an overhead waterwheel. Beginning to get it? How about the room in which we stayed, the Daisy Mae: The walls are rough-hewn boulders. So are the floors and ceilings, the shower and the washbasin. In fact, anything that can be a boulder is one. The only exceptions are the bed, the toilet, two night tables, the TV, and two strands of daisylike light fixtures. The boulder sink has no waterspouts. You turn the tap and hear a gurgling overhead to one side. Then down over the rocks and out from two little waterfalls come the hot and cold torrents. The shower works the same way. The inn's dining room is all pink—and that means all pink, right down to the cash register tapes. No pane of glass in the place that isn't stained or etched. No length of wood uncarved or unturned. No public wall that isn't a mural. Each of the hundred or so rooms is a different fantasy. Alex Madonna's castle is like a man so ugly he's handsome. Unlike Hearst's place, it should not be missed."           —*Mechtild Hoppenrath and Charles Oberdorf*

"The neglected fact about the famous Madonna Inn is that it's not so much a hotel as a motel. The rooms are often small, and in long rows, reachable from the outside. Somehow, when you realize that for all the kooky effects you're basically in a motel, a little goes out of the experience. But it's still a great experience, if you're in the mood. The trick is to enjoy the outrageously bad taste—so bad it's almost good—without looking down on the throngs (including legions of honeymooners) for whom it's an esthetic pinnacle. Mr. Madonna's sense of humor and his desire to beautify are quite affecting."           —*Tom Congdon*

"Pure, unadulterated kitsch."           —*Barbara Gollob*

"We tried to reserve ahead at the Madonna Inn, but they claimed on the phone to be fully booked, saying that we would be put on their waiting list and that, as twenty-fourth on that list, we had a good chance of getting in. So we motored up on the off-chance; the hotel indeed had a vacancy sign when we drove up. We looked the place over and then retired gratefully to a nearby motel. It's so very synthetic and plastic."           —*Hilary Rubinstein*

Open all year.
109 rooms, all with private bath.
Rates $60–$137.
No credit cards.

German, French, and Spanish spoken.
Manager: Billy Long

## Santa Barbara

### The Bath Street Inn
1720 Bath Street
Santa Barbara, California 93101
Telephone (805) 682-9680

"To quote from the brochure, this inn, close to the heart of old
Santa Barbara, offers the traditional warmth and hospitality of a
European bed-and-breakfast inn. The spacious house, once a residence, is run by Susan Brown and Nancy Stover, two friendly
women who are most helpful in making reservations and such. We
enjoyed a delicious continental breakfast of fresh orange juice,
homemade croissants, coffee cake, and steaming hot coffee, all
served in a cheery breakfast room."                —*Sarah McBride*

Open all year.
6 rooms, 2 with private bath.
Rates $50–$85, depending on season, including continental break-
    fast.
Credit cards: MasterCard, Visa.
Innkeepers: Susan P. Brown and Nancy Stover.

### Glenborough Inn
1327 Bath Street
Santa Barbara, California 93101
Telephone (805) 966-0589

"The Glenborough is the most charming and elegant inn we have
stayed in. There are four lovely rooms in the main inn and four
more across the street in the Cottage. We especially enjoyed the
New Orleans-style garden under a huge tree at the Cottage. The
private hot tub is a welcome respite after a day of sightseeing or
shopping. We also have stayed in the green and white plant-
decorated Garden Room, the autumn-toned Country Room, and
the Captain's Quarters, with its genuine ship's wardrobe. One
breakfast, served in our room, was typical—chilled fresh juice,
baked fresh pear, fluffy biscuits with jam, coffee and tea."
                                              —*Louise M. Laub*

Open all year.
6 rooms, 2 suites, 4 with private bath.
Rates $40–$100, lower September to May, including breakfast in bed or in the garden.
Credit cards: MasterCard, Visa.
Innkeepers: Jo Ann Bell and Pat Hardy.

---

**The Upham Hotel**
1404 De La Vina
Santa Barbara, California 93101
Telephone (805) 962-0098

"The hotel was very calm and quiet, which was unexpected because it is so near the main downtown area. My room was off a small garden, decorated in Victorian style, although not fully antique. At dinner I overheard the manager saying that Julia Child was coming the next week for brunch. It was very pleasant, much nicer than the Sheraton, where I usually stay in Santa Barbara."
—*Dr. Thomas Lechtenberg*

Open all year.
50 rooms, all with private bath.
Rates $75–$115, including continental breakfast.
Credit cards: MasterCard, Visa.
French, Italian, and Spanish spoken.
Innkeepers: Frieda Lawrence and Julie Henning.

---

**Casa Madrona**
801 Bridgeway
Sausalito, California
Telephone: (415) 332-0502

"A lovely, old Victorian-style inn, located on a hill overlooking the San Francisco Bay. I had a gorgeous view of the boats out in the water early in the morning with the sun coming up. They also have a fine dining room (expensive) with someone playing the piano. It was a very enjoyable stay. The house was built in 1885 as the private residence of lumber baron William G. Barrett."    —*Mary Pognono*

Open all year.
29 rooms, 28 with private bath, 3 suites.

Rates $63.50–$121.90, including continental breakfast.
Credit cards: American Express, MasterCard, Visa.
Dining room and bar.
German spoken.
Innkeeper: John Mays.

## Seal Beach

**The Old Seal Beach Inn**
212 5th Street
Seal Beach, California 90740
Telephone (213) 493-2416

"A mediocre motel has been renovated with great charm—blue awnings, brick courtyard, old ironwork fences and lightposts have changed a run-of-the-mill motor court into a really delightful spot. Within walking distance of the beach and the town, the Old Seal Beach Inn is near the Long Beach marina, an easy drive to Disneyland and the Los Alamitos racetrack. Most units have kitchenettes. There is a pool, a library, and a bridal suite. Continental breakfast is served in the library and may be eaten at poolside or in one's room. We had plenty of freshly squeezed orange juice, tasty (but cold) Danish, and coffee in—alas—a styrofoam cup. It's still a charming, delightful place with a very friendly staff. No TVs or phones—super privacy. Lots and lots of TLC—flowers everywhere. Located in a quiet residential neighborhood."     —*N. Kennedy*

Open all year.
24 rooms, all with private bath.
Rates $42–$60, suites $75–$90, including continental breakfast.
Limited Chinese and Spanish spoken.
Credit cards: American Express, MasterCard, Visa.
Manager: Bruce Hovland.

## Sonoma

**Sonoma Chalet**
18935 Fifth Street West
Sonoma, California 95476
Telephone (707) 938-3129

"A wonderful country-farm setting. The country breakfast served each morning by the hosts is even cooked on a wood stove. As you enter the Chalet, you are taken back in time to the late 1800s or early

1900s. Very charming, very antique. Complimentary wine and fruit are served in the parlor rooms.'' —*Sharon Haugen-Dix*

Open all year.
4 rooms, 1 cottage, 1 with private bath.
Rates $55 double, $75 cottage, including full breakfast.
No credit cards.
Innkeepers: Lolita and Patrick Murphy.

_____ *Sutter Creek*

**Nine Eureka Street**
P.O. Box 386
Sutter Creek, California 95685
Telephone (209) 267-0342

"There are several good reasons for visiting northern California's gold country: its beautiful rolling highlands, the nostalgic aura of the gold rush days that pervades the small Western towns of the Mother Lode, and the unique experience of unwinding at Nine Eureka Street in Sutter Creek. The spacious sitting room, with its interesting memorabilia and wonderful collection of books, is meant for lingering. The guest rooms are a delight to the connoisseur of the past—each as individual in feeling and decor as only the inn's proprietress (no novice in the art of innkeeping) could have fashioned. For those who read in bed, she has provided excellent lighting, as well as a galaxy of reading material. At breakfast time, guests gather in the sunlit dining room to find a table refreshingly laid with elegant silver and china. Fresh orange juice in a tall crystal pitcher, slices of melon or other fruit, homemade bread and pastry, with steaming coffee, are complimentary—and a happy start to a day of browsing in the numerous antique shops of Sutter Creek, or exploring nearby Jackson, Mokelumne Hill, Ione, Volcano, Amador City, Fiddletown, and other historic attractions of the gold country." —*Rita F. Murphy*

Open all year.
5 rooms, 4 with private bath.
Rates $45–$60, including continental breakfast.
No credit cards.
Amada Stage Line buses from Sacramento.
Innkeeper: Marie Sanders.

Turn to the back of this book for pages inviting *your* comments.

**Sutter Creek Inn**
75 Main Street (Box 385)
Sutter Creek, California 95685
Telephone (209) 267-5606

"In a warren of buildings behind the 1859 Keyes-Voorhies home, Jane Way installed a series of hideaway accommodations. Each is individually decorated with odd pieces of comfortable modern furniture. Some units have beds suspended on chains. Sleeping on a swinging bed gives much of the pleasure of a hammock with none of the spine-bending discomfort. It is also more predictable and less active than a water bed. The nonadventurous may use blocks provided to stabilize the furniture.

"Established in 1966, the inn was one of the first modern country inns to open in California. Each room is furnished with a carafe of California sherry, and those who get to the dining room before the breakfast bell may pour brandy into their morning coffee. A hearty hot breakfast is served at long tables in the main house, and the assembled guests become an instant extended family, united in their pursuit of sightseeing the Mother Lode country. Abandoned gold mines, toppled tailing wheels, and ancient Indian village sites are to be explored. In Amador City a museum (erratic hours, check ahead) houses working-scale models of mine structures. If you travel between March 24 and April 21, a drive past Daffodil Hill near Volcano should be enjoyable. In winter there is snowmobiling and skiing."
—*Camille J. Cook; also recommended by Sue Swezey*

Open all year, except weekdays in January.
18 rooms, all with private bath.
Rates $35–$72, including "sit-down" breakfast.
No credit cards.
Bus service from Sacramento.
Innkeeper: Jane Way.

## *Yosemite*

**Ahwahnee Hotel**
Yosemite National Park, California 95389
Telephone (209) 373-4171

"At the bottom of the valley's verdant floor, hard by the Merced River, which is fed by Yosemite Falls—and previously, a series of ramified glaciers—is the Ahwahnee Hotel. Made of fieldstone and redwood in 1927, it has just the right number of rooms for a mutuality of convenience and privacy. Despite its location near the heart of one of America's most visited national parks, the guest feels a sense of tranquillity and elegance when entering the stone gates abutting the hotel's entrance. The Ahwahnee's food is grandly served in a handsome cathedral-ceilinged dining room with a view of Glacier Point. Fastidious care has been taken in the preparation of the food enjoyed by guests, be they overnighters or in residence for such an occasion as the legendary days of Christmas.

"The six-story structure—which seems ever so squat and homey in contrast to the perpendicular walls nearby—has received and housed a near-legendary number of presidents, let alone emperors and kings. It has been said that such a critic as Frank Lloyd Wright found it to be grand yet not imperious. The Ahwahnee is comfortable for the weekender who wants to get away from urban tensions. The naturalist, in search of the Sierra Nevadas' unique flora and fauna, or the unabashed romantic is likely to be thrilled to the bottom of his socks by the four (or are they really five?) waterfalls nearby: Yosemite (made up of two falls) and Bridalveil, Vernal, and Ribbon. It is all very, very awesome. Truly, there, within the Ahwahnee's great halls, its game room, or along one of its great loggias, one finds a special respect for space and proportion. At the Ahwahnee, man seems to be decidedly at peace with his environment."

—*Dr. F. M. Hinkhouse*

Open all year.
121 rooms, all with private bath.
Rates $119–$140. AP available.
Credit cards: American Express, Diners Club, MasterCard, Visa.
Yosemite Transportation System buses to and from Merced several times daily link travelers with Golden Gate Airways, Amtrak, or Greyhound and Trailways buses. Bus service is expanded in summer to include Fresno and Lee Vining.
Manager: John O'Neill.

## *Yountville*

**Burgundy and Bordeaux House**
6711 Washington Street (Box 2766)
Yountville, California 94599
Telephone (707) 944-2855

Set in the heart of the Napa Valley wine country, this inn with its thick stone walls was built in the 1870s, and was originally a brandy works.

"There are some fine country French antiques in this inn. We had a large bedroom with French doors and a bath—a deluxe suite. Although they serve only breakfast, there was a good Italian restaurant next door that served good homemade pastas and sauces."

—*Nell Thomas*

Open all year.
14 rooms, 11 with private bath.
Rates: Subject to change; call or write for current rates.
Credit cards: American Express, Diners Club, MasterCard, Visa.
Spanish spoken.
Greyhound buses to Yountville. Evans airport service to San Francisco.
Innkeeper: Mary Keenan.

---

**Magnolia Hotel**
6529 Yount Street (P.O. Drawer M)
Yountville, California 94599
Telephone (707) 944-2056

This handsome stone building, built in 1873 as a hotel, was used at one stage (according to the present owners, Bruce and Bonnie Locken) as a bordello. The hotel has a swimming pool, a Jacuzzi spa, and a restaurant (open Friday and Saturday only) whose wine cellar boasts a selection of over 200 wines. The inn, in fact, overlooks vineyards.

"Each room is different and is filled with French antiques. The dining room is small, beautifully intimate, and very French in feeling, with crystal candleholders and lace tablecloths."

—*Nell Thomas*

Open all year.
11 rooms, all with private bath.
Rates $65–$135, including full breakfast.
No credit cards.
Greyhound buses to Yountville.
Innkeepers: Bruce and Bonnie Locken.

Where are the good little hotels in Boston? Philadelphia? Omaha? Dallas? If you have found one, don't keep it a secret. Write *now*.

# Hawaii

## Hawaii Volcanoes National Park

**Volcano House**
Hawaii Volcanoes National Park, Hawaii 96718
Telephone (808) 967-7321

"In the chill of morning, steam rises from the dark crater. The sun begins to come up over the primitive rain forest of tree ferns and oddly twisted ohia trees. Pele, the ancient volcano goddess, sleeps peacefully in her home in Kilauea Crater. High in the mountains of Hawaii, the big island, it doesn't look like those travel posters with sand, surf, and palm trees. This is another Hawaii.

"Volcano House, perched right on the edge of the crater, is now owned by the Sheraton chain, but it retains the homey, mountain hunting-lodge charm created by former owner George Lycurgus. Rooms are pleasant, clean, and comfortable but simple and of moderate size. Many have windows overlooking the crater itself. Evenings are cool, and a fire in the large fireplace in the main public room is much appreciated. Guests can watch movies of a recent volcanic eruption, shown on a 16mm sound projector in an adjoining room, or bathe in volcano steam in the tiled steam room, which has both a shower and a deep, Japanese-style tub.

"At midday Volcano House is a favorite lunch stop for tourist buses between Kona and Hilo, and the dining room overlooking the crater can get very crowded. At breakfast and dinner, however, you don't have to battle crowds of tourists. Dusk is the best time to watch the sunset over the crater. Dinners are beautifully served, with a fresh orchid on each plate, and the food is very good. Try the mahimahi with chopped macadamia nuts; it may well be the best served anywhere in the state, and mahimahi, a fish native to Hawaiian waters, seems to be on nearly every menu.

"The original Volcano House, in use from 1864 until construction of the present building, is just a short walk across the road. It has been turned into a community art center. The original bedrooms are now studios for local artists, and the public rooms have become galleries for the paintings, drawings, wood carvings, weavings, photography, and other arts produced here. Items are all for sale; prices are reasonable and quality high. The day we were there a Hawaiian language lesson was in progress on the wide porch that stretches across the front of the art center.

"Paved trails allow visitors to walk along the rim of the volcano to the ohia forest, to lava deposits, to a huge crack caused by an earthquake. A two-lane road circles the crater with many spots to stop to observe the activity, whether it be merely rising steam or something more dramatic. The Halemaumau fire pit is a crater within the crater. When you drive to the edge of Halemaumau, you are actually inside Kilauea Crater at its most active spot. Here you can see deposits of yellow sulfuric rock and smell the pungent odor of sulfur.

"A 72-par golf course presents problems that golfers seldom find elsewhere. Other nearby attractions include the Mauna Loa macadamia plantation with special free tours, and Kalapana and Punalu'u black sand beaches, all just a short drive from Volcano House."

*—JLS*

"The view over the crater is a compelling magnet for your attention, a primeval landscape you probably can't encounter with equal convenience anyplace else on earth. If you don't get a room facing the crater, then spend some time in the bar, where you will be bewitched by the curls of smoke rising from the open gash in the earth's skin just outside the bar's wide windows. A local concoction, the Halemaumau, is a vigorous rum drink of nice balance. Don't miss a walk through the lava tube when you're in the area."

*—Camille J. Cook*

Open all year.
37 rooms, all with private bath.
Rates $37–$48 double.

Credit cards: American Express, Carte Blanche, Diners Club, En
   Route, MasterCard, Visa.
Japanese spoken.
Innkeeper: Alec Dizol.

_____*Honolulu*

**Colony Surf**
2895 Kalakaua Avenue
Honolulu, Hawaii 96815
Telephone (808) 923-5751

"Waikiki has become a concrete jungle of hotels and condominiums
reaching to the sky. The sidewalks are crowded. Hotels fill every
available inch of land and construction is still going on. We chose
to stay in the Colony Surf on the beach at the foot of Diamond Head.
The crisp white of the woodwork and the spring green of the carpeting and wallpaper create a refreshing and serene atmosphere. We
had an eleventh-floor suite, an airy and sunny place with an immense window running along the whole width of the ocean side. A
floral arrangement in a silver bowl added an uncommercial touch
that we found to be true throughout our stay.

"The hotel is not inexpensive, but it offers many advantages that
make it far superior to a room on the beach at Waikiki. The suites
are equipped with kitchenettes fully stocked with dishes, flatware,
cooking utensils, refrigerator, gas stove, and dishwasher. There is
a little grocery store around the corner. Bus fare anywhere in town
is not costly. A few steps away from the Colony Surf is the Colony
East, where you will find smaller accommodations, though still suit-
able for families. That building is not on the beach, but overlooks
a park and Diamond Head.

"Dining at the Colony Surf is an adventure in fine cuisine.
Michel's is an award-winning restaurant and richly deserves its reputation. The atmosphere is that of an elegant French dining room
with crystal chandeliers, period furniture, and formally attired waiters. The view of the beach and the ocean is unrestricted.

—*Louisa L. Becker*

Open all year.
100 rooms, all with private bath.
Rates $70–$500.
Credit cards: American Express, Carte Blanche, Diners Club, MasterCard, Visa.

French, German, Japanese, Spanish, and Chinese spoken.
Innkeeper: Judy Daniel.

## Kailua-Kona

### Kona Village Resort
Box 1299
Kailua-Kona, Hawaii 96740
Telephone (808) 325-5555

"Kona Village Resort is a collection of 95 *hales,* or Polynesian thatch-roofed houses, built along the shores of Kahuwai Bay among the ancient Hawaiian fishponds which remain from the village of Kaupulehu. An 1801 eruption of the now-extinct volcano Hualalai devastated much of the surrounding area with its lava flow, but the flow miraculously moved around Kahuwai Bay, sparing a jewel of a white-sanded, palm-treed crescent. Here, amid the remnants of an ancient Hawaiian settlement of the *alii,* or royalty, sits Kona Village.

"Visitors enjoy a rest from the real world—no bells, no keys, no telephones. Daily costs include room and three meals a day, scuba equipment, snorkels, sunfish sailboats, tennis courts, shuffleboard, ping-pong, a putting green, swimming pool, fishing equipment.

"Breakfast and dinner are served in the dining room, built in the form of a New Hebrides island long house. The food is quite good with the exception of desserts, which are universally disappointing. Lunch is served on the flagstone patio—a sumptuous buffet with an array of local delicacies and fruits.

"Resort activities, which change daily, include hikes to collect puka shells for necklaces, coconut basket weaving, ancient hula demonstrations, Hawaiian quilting lessons. Staff members take guests to see the ancient petroglyphs located on the resort's fifteen acres.

"For a total escape from the twentieth century and a relaxing look at old Hawaii with the comforts of today, Kona Village Resort can not be equaled!"                            —*Margaret Ziegler*

Open all year, except end of November to mid-December.
95 thatched bungalows *(hales),* 24 of which are suites, all with private bath.
Rates $210–$340 per couple per day, AP, including recreational facilities and equipment.
Credit cards: All accepted.
General Manager: Fred Duerr.

# Nevada

## Virginia City

**The Gold Hill Hotel**
P.O. Box 304
Virginia City, Nevada 89440
Telephone (702) 847-0111

"On entering Gold Canyon, flamboyant with color in the fall, the little town of the Gold Hill whisks you back to the era of the gold and silver kings of the 1870s and 1880s. Many of the buildings are gone, of course, the victims of strong winds, heavy snows, and desert sun—not to mention souvenir hunters. Prospectors began rushing the area in 1859, with the discovery of the great Comstock Lode, and it was well on its way to fame and fortune. On May 1 of that year, Vesey's Boarding House sprang up on the main street. The two-story building of mellowed brick and wood with white-painted railings still lends the charm of the pioneer West. Only its name and owners have changed over the years. The Gold Hill Hotel is now owned by Fred and Dorothy Immoor, who celebrated their twentieth anniversary at the hotel in 1978. The hotel snuggles against the sagebrush-covered hills within the shadows of the Crown Point Trestle, where millions in gold and silver ore were shipped to the mills on the Carson River by the Virginia and Truckee Railroad."                                    —*Dorothy Paulsen*

"The small hotel has six rooms, a banquet room for weddings, and the old original bar where the overnight guests gather to talk or cook their own steaks. Up the rock-walled stairway there's a community bathroom with a chilly stone floor and an old-fashioned bathtub. The bridal suite at the end of the hall has a four-poster bed and a turn-of-the-century picture of Cupid on the pink walls. The other rooms are furnished with period pieces from Virginia City and the Gold Hill area. Morning brings the sun and the smell of coffee into your room. Guests are greeted downstairs by Dorothy's delicious brew and Fred's good-natured banter. They tell you how they've raised four children while acknowledging their years of labor. You realize the significance of the sign outside: 'This is the first edifice known to Nevada to be worthy of the name hotel.' "
                          —*Jim Beazley; also recommended by Wilbur E. Wieprecht*

Open all year.
6 rooms with shared baths.
Rate $25.
No credit cards.
Nearest airports: Reno and Lake Tahoe. Buses and trains to Reno.
Innkeeper: Terry Immoor.

Details of special features offered by an inn or hotel vary according to information supplied by the hotels themselves. The absence here of a recreational amenity, a bar, or a restaurant doesn't necessarily mean one of these doesn't exist. Ask the innkeeper when booking your room.

# Utah

## Midway

**The Homestead**
700 North Homestead Drive
Midway, Utah 84049
Telephone (801) 654-1102

"A number of buildings make up the Homestead—the Virginian
House, the Farmhouse, the Ranch House, the Barn, the Mill House,
Valley View, and the Guest House. It is like an old farmyard with
cottages. The Homestead, at an altitude of 6,000 feet, is east of Salt
Lake City, near the Park City recreation area. There are thermal
pools, known as 'hot pots,' with temperatures between 85 and 92
degrees." —*Jack Goodman*

Open all year.
44 rooms, all with private bath.
Rates $39–$54.
Credit cards: American Express, MasterCard, Visa.
Nearest airport: Salt Lake City, 45 minutes away.
Innkeepers: Carl and Melba Morgan.

_____*Salt Lake City*

## Carlton Hotel
140 East South Temple Street
Salt Lake City, Utah 84111
Telephone (801) 355-3418

"A clean, inexpensive hotel, well located in the historic downtown area of the city. A favorite with European visitors, it is rather an ordinary-looking building of red brick and white-painted pillars. Neat but not gaudy. There's no bar but there is a coffee shop."

—*Jack Goodman*

Open all year.
80 rooms, 46 with private bath.
Rates $26 single, $36 double.
Credit cards: American Express, MasterCard, Visa.
2 blocks from Greyhound terminal, 3 blocks from Amtrak station. Bus from airport.
Innkeeper: James Wright.

## Hotel Utah
Main at South Temple
Salt Lake City, Utah 84111
Telephone (801) 531-1000

"Directly across the broad treelined street from Temple Square is a wonderful hostelry which is at the figurative crossroads of the West. The rooms are large and decidedly cheerful and the food of the first order. Hotel Utah is a prize property of the Church of Jesus Christ of Latter-Day Saints.

"From the restaurant on top of the white Second Empire structure, you can sit at your banquette and feast your eyes on the spires and the sculpture of the Angel Moroni atop the adjacent Mormon Temple. In a sense it is almost as if you had a prized window table at Paris's Tour d'Argent when your host has paid the required fee to the verger to light the Cathedral of Notre Dame in your honor, and presumably for the well-being of your soul. A classic menu will be proffered. I, for one, have long opted for the borscht, which has been on the menu for decades. Likewise, the bread is magnificent and seemingly endless in its variety. The vegetables are steamed to the appropriate minimal point. Until my visit to the Utah, I had not realized that squash came in so many forms and colors—or that it could be so delectable.

"The Mormon Church does not brook the sale of alcohol on the premises. That, however, does not halt the brown-baggers who are not intimidated by the church's ukase."      —*Dr. F. M. Hinkhouse*

Open all year.
500 rooms, all with private bath.
Rates $59 single, $69 double, $89–$465 suites.
Credit cards: American Express, Carte Blanche, Diners Club, MasterCard, Visa.
Many languages spoken.
Manager: Stuart G. Cross.

Do you know a hotel in your state that we have overlooked? Write *now.*

# Part Two

## Plains, Northwest, and Alaska

*Alaska*
*Idaho*
*Montana*
*North Dakota*
*Oregon*
*South Dakota*
*Washington*
*Wyoming*

# _Alaska_

## Skagway

**Skagway Inn**
Seventh and Broadway (Box 483 W)
Skagway, Alaska 99840
Telephone (907) 983-2289

"Skagway today boasts a population of 750, reduced somewhat from the 10,000 people who swelled the town during the gold rush of 1898. The main street is almost unchanged, with its Pack Train Saloon, the Arctic Brotherhood Hall, the Golden North Hotel, and the White Pass and Yukon Railroad depot. The National Park Service has carefully restored a few buildings, seeking to maintain the frontier spirit of Soapy Smith and his gang.

"The Skagway Inn has the charm of its locale and the warmth of home. Rooms are named for infamous ladies of the good old days. A player piano in excellent working condition graces the living room. Coffee and homemade pastries are put out every morning for guests. A highly recommended hotel, and the cheapest in town to boot." —_Jean Carlton Parker_

Open all year.
15 rooms with shared baths.

Rates $37–$42, including continental breakfast.
Credit cards: MasterCard, Visa.
Air, bus, ferry, and cruise ship service. Guests met at terminals and
port.
Innkeepers: Wendell and Frances Long.

Would you be so kind as to share discoveries you may have of
charming, well-run places to stay in Europe? Please write to *Europe's
Wonderful Little Hotels and Inns,* c/o Congdon & Weed, 298 Fifth
Avenue, New York, New York 10001. (By the way, a new and greatly
expanded edition of this splendid guide is now available at your
bookseller's.)

# Idaho

## Boise

**The Idanha**
Main Street at 10th
Boise, Idaho 83702
Telephone (208) 342-3611

Idaho became a state in 1890, opening the way to further growth for an area already rich in mining and on the verge of a canal-building era that would turn more and more land into productive acreage. Boise, the state's capital, needed a new hotel.

"The Idanha is the outstanding example of the French château style of architecture in the state. This nationally registered landmark opened as a luxury hotel on the first day of the twentieth century, and its castlelike towers still grace Main Street. Handsomely restored to its original elegance, the Idanha today features Rolls-Royce limousine service, Victorian accommodations, and Peter Schott's continental restaurant."          —*Arthur A. Hart*

Open all year.
100 rooms, 65 with private bath.

Rates $30 single, $40 double.
Credit cards: American Express, Diners Club, MasterCard, Visa.
Limousine service to Boise Municipal Airport.
Manager: Calvin Jensen.

American hotels and inns generally list rates by the room, assuming
one person in a single, two in a double. Extra people in rooms
normally incur extra charges. Where rates are quoted per person
per day, at least one meal is probably included under a Modified
American plan (MAP). A full American Plan (AP) would include
three meals.

# _Montana_

## Essex

**Izaak Walton Inn**
Box 653
Essex, Montana 59916
Telephone: Ask operator for Essex Number 1

"The inn, just off Highway 2 on the southern boundary of Glacier National Park, is surrounded by scenic mountains and a million acres of wilderness. It is obvious that it was built to serve the railroad that passes right by the door, though trains no longer stop here. A couple of dozen immaculate but austere rooms provide visitors with a feeling that they have been transported back into the 1920s. Each room has rugs rather than carpeting, a porcelain sink, more than adequate closet space, and central bathrooms down the hall a few paces. Part of the charm of staying at the Izaak Walton is bumping into other lodgers, wrapped in towels, heading for a morning or evening bath. Later in the evening, in the elegant basement bar, these lodgers join in revelry that lasts well into the night. Meals are essentially family style, with closely spaced tables in a quaintly furnished dining area immediately adjacent to a large, comfortably appointed fireplace room, a gathering place for hikers and skiers.

"One is struck by the simple wooden architecture of the inn. Inside there are varnished floors, beamed ceilings, and a rock fireplace. Throughout the building there are touches of a railroad-station theme. This is best exemplified in the bar, a museum of railroad memorabilia. A recent addition to the inn includes a large conference room, beneath which is located a huge sauna. The sauna adds an entirely new luster to the end of a hiking, fishing, or skiing day.

"Breakfasts are traditional affairs, designed to satiate the appetites of outdoorsmen: huge pancakes, thick slices of cured bacon, fresh eggs, and steaming pots of coffee. Evening meals concentrate on great quantities of beef, chicken, or pork with all the trimmings.

"The inn also serves as post office for a widely dispersed population of hardy Montanans who have retreated from more crowded sections of the region. They come to eat, drink, chat, rent ski equipment, arrange for river float trips on the Middle Fork of the Flathead River, but mostly to stop by the place that is the cracker barrel of western Montana. Informality is the rule. Leave your suits and ties at home, and bring jeans, hiking and riding boots, and the gear needed to enjoy the great northern Rocky Mountains."

—*Richard A. Solberg*

Open all year.
28 rooms, 4 with private bath.
Rates $26 double, $35 double deluxe.
Credit cards: MasterCard, Visa.
Public restaurant and bar.
Nearest train at Whitefish, 40 miles away.
Innkeepers: Larry and Lynda Vielleux.

---

*Pray*

**Chico Hot Springs**
Pray, Montana 59065
Telephone (406) 333-4411; 333-4490

"Chico Hot Springs has been easing the sore muscles of visitors since the 1860s, when the Yellowstone Valley was first settled as part of the Emigrant Peak gold find. The hotel and pool were built about 1900 as a health spa. Chico is still the place to soak out the tensions of twentieth-century business. To people from the megalopoli of the East and West coasts, everything in Montana must appear small. But when you go there, look up at the sky: it really is bigger.

"Chico can be used as a headquarters for side trips into the natural scenery or historic sites of Montana. Custer battlefield and Indian reservation are one such trip. Another trip might be to the Historical Museum in the state capital of Helena, which has a large collection of Charles M. Russell paintings. Still another visit might be to Butte, once the richest hill on earth; it has much turn-of-the-century architecture. Yellowstone and Grand Teton parks are also nearby, as are the Yellowstone River and its famous trout.

"At the hotel, you may stay in the original rooms or in new motel units. Twenty-five years ago, Chico served hamburgers in the dining room. Now the menu is one to make a restaurant in a large city proud. Try the barbecued bones (beef ribs in sauce). Before you go, you might ask if you can play the Steinway grand in the lobby."

*—Judge Paul Buchanan*

Open all year.

57 rooms, 9 with private bath; 12 motel units, 2 condominiums, 3 cabins, all with private bath.

Rates $30–$36 for rooms and motel units, $55 for cabins, $90–$110 for condominium units, which sleep 6 or 10.

Credit cards: MasterCard, Visa.

Restaurant and bar.

Manager: Janet Thurman.

Details of special features offered by an inn or hotel vary according to information supplied by the hotels themselves. The absence here of a recreational amenity, a bar, or a restaurant doesn't necessarily mean one of these doesn't exist. Ask the innkeeper when booking your room.

# North Dakota

## Medora

**The Rough Riders**
Medora, North Dakota 58645
Telephone (701) 623-4422

"Around the little town of Medora in the North Dakota Badlands is some of the most spectacular natural scenery in the world. The barren bluffs and buttes, with layers of the earth's history exposed, and the deep, shaded ravines carved by the Little Missouri River, are a startling contrast to the prairie. The muted colors, the layers of soil, and the textures are beautiful in any light. Medora has been restored to the time when Theodore Roosevelt raised cattle in the area and the Marquis de Mores had a grand plan for a packing plant to process the local beef. The hotel is the center of the town, and it is just as it was when Teddy Roosevelt was a guest—complete with wooden sidewalk.

"The hotel is constructed inside and out of rough lumber that has been left unpainted. You feel you are in a true cow town when you climb the center stairway leading to the antique-furnished rooms. All this is juxtaposed with a fine menu in a dining room that could be expected only in a city. Mornings at the Rough Riders are a delight. The rugged old buttes and incredibly clear sky, with the sounds of breakfast downstairs, make you aware of how fine a way this is to begin a day."                              —*Carol Winger*

"This is a good place to stay and to eat, and it breaks up the monotony of traveling through this part of the country."
                                                —*Mark L. Goodman*

Open Memorial Day to Labor Day.
9 rooms, plus motel annex, all with private bath.
Rate $41.50 double.
Credit cards: American Express, MasterCard, Visa.
Manager: John Conway.

Turn to the back of this book for pages inviting *your* comments.

*Jacksonville Inn,*
*Jacksonville*

# Oregon

## Ashland

**Ashland Hills Inn**
2525 Ashland Street
Ashland, Oregon, 97520
Telephone (503) 482-8310

This rambling, motel-style inn is not old, but it has been built to conform nicely with its natural surroundings. Much use is made of wood and other natural materials. Ashland has a summer Shakespeare festival.

"The Ashland Hills Inn serves a small college town and the entire Rogue River Valley. The food here is superb, and the guest list fascinating, for it is made up of actors and others who are on the boards or attending the Oregon Shakespeare Festival or the Peter Britt Musical Series. Conversation never seems to pall. The inn takes care of town and gown as well as ranchers and lumber tycoons who seem to use it as their club."     —*Dr. F. M. Hinkhouse*

Open all year.
159 rooms and suites, all with private bath.
Rates $55–$78.

Credit cards: American Express, Diners Club, MasterCard, Visa.
Danish, French, German, Italian, and Spanish spoken.
Nearest airport at Medford, 15 miles away.
Innkeeper: Hans J. Boldt.

# Cottage Grove

## The Village Green
725 Row River Road (P.O. Box 277)
Cottage Grove, Oregon 97424
Telephone (503) 942-2491

"There are few spots in Oregon along I-5 that are of singular interest for those in need of food and rest. The Village Green is an
exception. Situated in a bosky part of a rich agricultural valley, this
small resort has become an oasis for the driver journeying between
San Francisco and Seattle. There is lots to do at the Village Green,
with its handsome rooms, elegant dining room, cozy bar, and piano-
shaped swimming pool. Golf and tennis are nearby; there is bowling
on the green. Once a year there is the Concours d'Elegance, a show
for classic automobiles. There is also the beloved Goose, the only
authentic excursion steam train in the Northwest. The visitor can
take a two-and-a-half-hour round-trip chug on the Goose to the
historic Bohemia Mines, a famed gold-mining lode of a gone but not
forgotten era. The tree and flower varieties along the route are
seemingly limitless. They are as much a treat to the eye as the hotel's
blueberry pancakes are to the stomach—something I heartily advise
enjoying before setting off for those hills."

*—Dr. F. M. Hinkhouse*

Open all year.
86 rooms, 10 suites, all with private bath.
Rates $40–$45 double, $65–$110 suites.
Credit cards: American Express, Carte Blanche, Diners Club, Mas-
terCard, Visa.
Bar, coffee shop, and dining room.
Greyhound buses serve Cottage Grove. Air and train service to
Eugene.
Danish, Dutch, and German spoken.
General Manager: Loy Helmly.

Where are the good little hotels in Boston? Philadelphia? Omaha?
Dallas? If you have found one, don't keep it a secret. Write *now.*

## Depoe Bay

**Channel House**
Box 49
Depoe Bay, Oregon 97341
Telephone (503) 765-2140

"The ocean is in your backyard, and there is a huge deck for watching fishing boats coming and going. There are woodburning fireplaces, warm comforters, candy mints on pillows, and a hot tub in one unit. A very good restaurant is down below. All rooms have color TV, FM radio, and HBO movie channels."

—*Maggi White*

Open all year.
7 rooms and suites, all with private bath.
Rates $35–$112, according to size and view.
No credit cards.
Air Oregon serves Newport, 12 miles away. Greyhound buses stop in Depoe Bay.
Innkeeper: Paul Schwabe.

## Gleneden Beach

**Salishan Lodge**
Gleneden Beach, Oregon 97388
Telephone (503) 764-3600

"Salishan Lodge is a modern hotel overlooking the Pacific Ocean and, more particularly, Siletz Bay. Each of its capacious rooms has its own fireplace and an adequate supply of wood. 'Cozy contemporary' might best describe the look. The Gray family, who did not stint when it came to taste in furnishing the hotel, are great art collectors and champions of the art of the Pacific Northwest. The lodge is dramatically situated in a deep, dark forest of Douglas fir, hemlock, and alder. Handsome carved walkways give access to a dining room, sunny coffee shop, an attic bar, and recreation facilities that include an indoor swimming pool, gyms, saunas, hydrotherapy pool, and indoor tennis courts. Adjacent to the '19th Hole' is an eighteen-hole championship golf course. On one side of the links is a private airstrip; on the other, a series of endless beaches that beckon the hiker."                    —*Dr. F. M. Hinkhouse*

Open all year.
150 rooms and suites, all with private bath.

Rates $74–$118 (may vary seasonally).
Credit cards: American Express, Carte Blanche, Diners Club, MasterCard, Visa.
Nearest airport at Portland. Some bus service available.
General manager: Russ Cleveland.

## Gold Beach

**Tu Tu Tun Lodge**
96550 North Bank Rogue
Gold Beach, Oregon 97444
Telephone (503) 247-6664

"There are so many things to enjoy about this attractive lodge on the Rogue River: large, comfortable rooms supplied with current magazines and fresh flowers; gourmet meals served at round tables; a pool for swimming and relaxing; nightly outside fires; conversations with guests from various parts of the United States and around the world; jet-boat trips on the river; ocean and river fishing. All this is orchestrated by personable innkeepers."      —*Jack and Sue Lane*

Open May 1 to October 31.
16 rooms, 2 river suites, all with private bath.
Rates $73 double, $86–$91 suites.
Credit cards: MasterCard, Visa.
Innkeepers: Dirk and Laurie Van Zante.

## Government Camp

**Timberline Lodge**
Government Camp, Oregon 97028
Telephone (503) 226-7979; 272-3311 or toll-free in Idaho, Nevada, Utah, Northern California, and Washington (800) 547-1406; toll-free in Oregon (800) 452-1335

"The day that Franklin Delano Roosevelt drove up from Portland to the slopes of Mount Hood to dedicate the Timberline Lodge must have been a happy one for him. His grand tour of the West had been a great success. He had been able to take the Union Pacific Railroad to the coast, see a unified nation at work during World War II, and enjoy pleasures he most delighted in. Timberline Lodge at Government Camp was a project close to his heart. In taste, it was to become a bellwether for ski resorts. Masons, craftsmen, carpenters, and artisans of many persuasions collected for this WPA project, lived and worked together here in an extraordinary freemasonry of art. What they achieved at the lodge was unique for the highly populist society of their time.

"Despite subsequent changes in taste, the lodge is still respected for its design and decor. Its style beggars any facile categorization. The scale of the lodge is monumental: it is nearly 400 feet long, four stories in elevation, and is dominated by a cupola that is a poetic reflection of the summit of Mount Hood. Its cathedralesque grand hall reflects the Olympian aspect of its surroundings. In a sense, what sculptors carving gargoyles did for the great cathedrals of Europe, the craftsmen of Oregon did for the lodge. The newelposts are singular examples of their success. The rooms of the lodge are furnished with a special dated feeling. To some they may seem bland, reflecting the age of their creation. Others may find them campy." —*Dr. F. M. Hinkhouse*

Open all year.
56 rooms, all with private bath. Chalets also available.
Rates $30–$90 double.
Credit cards: American Express, MasterCard, Visa.
Transportation from Portland available by advance arrangement.
Innkeeper: Richard L. Kohnstamm.

_____*Hood River*

## Columbia Gorge Hotel
4000 West Cliff Drive
Hood River, Oregon 97031
Telephone (503) 386-5566

This is a 1920s hotel, and the jazz age has been restored here in everything from the furniture to the Art Nouveau menu cover featuring Sacajawea, the Indian woman who became the hero of Lewis and Clark's expedition to the Northwest. Food here is country Northwest, with Columbia River salmon and dry-aged Eastern prime beef as well as Hood River apple pie and apple blossom honey for the complimentary farm breakfast. The hotel is in a spectacular hillside setting, with the Columbia River at its feet and snow-covered Mount Hood behind it.

"A quiet, relaxing hotel established in 1921, and restored and reopened in 1979. Beautiful grounds. Excellent food. Good service. There are magnificent views of Columbia Gorge and the Columbia River. Nearby is a waterfall higher than Niagara."
—*Darrell and Diana Buell*

Open all year.
46 rooms, all with private bath.
Rates $38 single, $48–$110 double, including farm breakfast.
Credit cards: American Express, MasterCard, Visa.
Take exit 62 on I-84. Reachable also by train and Greyhound bus;
  ask inn for details.
Manager: Glen T. Brydges.

_____Jacksonville

**Jacksonville Inn**
175 East California Street (P.O. Box 359)
Jacksonville, Oregon 97530
Telephone (503) 899-1900

"Every year we make a pilgrimage to the Shakespeare festival in
Ashland. But where to stay? The answer for us is the Jacksonville
Inn, in the gold rush town of Jacksonville. The town's 1860s main
street has been restored—including the inn. Behind its brick facade
are eight rooms, all furnished with Victorian beds and lamps. Downstairs there is a large and attractive dining room with first-class
meals. The proprietor, Jerry Evans, is a wine buff as well as an
expert in Victoriana, and he has an impressive list of California
wines and several wines from Oregon. A comprehensive selection
of American and European wines is sold in the inn's roomy shop,
which displays a wide range of myrtle-wood objects.
  "On the outskirts of Jacksonville is Pioneer Village, a reconstruction of a dozen or so gold rush buildings and six covered wagons.
The reconstruction was the work of George McUne, a wheelwright
and wagon master who before his death led a commemorative trek
with his wagons along the Oregon Trail. Mr. McUne's widow and
son are continuing to show people around the village, which has a
good restaurant (dinners only) and old-fashioned, schmaltzy melo-
dramas on weekends. Many children visit Pioneer Village to see how
their forefathers and mothers lived."
                                    —*Dr. Joseph and Jane Wheelwright*

Open all year.
8 rooms, all with private bath.
Rates $35–$50.
Credit cards: American Express, Diners Club, MasterCard, Visa.
Public bar and restaurant.
Innkeepers: Jerry and Linda Evans.

# _____Oregon Caves National Monument

**Oregon Caves Chateau**
1439 Northeast 6 (P.O. Box 128)
Cave Junction, Oregon 97523
Telephone Oregon Caves toll station Number 1

An Oregonian named Elijah Davidson was hunting in the Siskiyou Mountains in fall 1874 when he saw a bear disappear into a mossy green hole high on a mountainside. Davidson's dog Bruno followed the bear, as a hunting dog should, and Davidson, in turn, followed his howling dog into a labyrinth of underground corridors. Dog and man emerged eventually; the bear remained. And so were discovered the Oregon Caves. It was not until 1907, when Joaquin Miller —who was known as the Poet of the Sierra—visited the caves and in his rapture called them the "marble halls of Oregon" that the public began to flock to this natural wonder, which is, in reality, only one cave, despite its name. In 1909, President Taft made this a national monument.

"In an unlikely situation, the Chateau was built during that halcyon period of government-sponsored architecture in the 1930s, when the Depression gave birth to the WPA and the Civilian Conservation Corps. The result is strangely wonderful. The lodge has almost the feeling of Ruritania about it, with its six-story cedar-bark sides. In the great hall, a cavernous fireplace capped by a vast, hoary slab of cedar dominates the distant far wall. It would seem to me to be the sort of rustic inn that William Randolph Hearst might have sought out.

"At the opposite end of the building, down a short flight of flagstone steps, is the Art Deco coffee shop, and just beyond that, the justly touted dining room. This is a generous space that one associates with a more leisurely society, when space was not yet considered a problem to utilize, to handle, to heat, or to cool. To further the effect, the dining room is bifurcated by a bubbling stream, called the River Styx underground in the magical world of trolls or gods and the decidedly more mundane Cave Creek when it comes to the surface.

"The food served in both the dining room and coffee shop is described by the park rangers as American cuisine, Josephine County variety. I would have to agree that it is down to earth, made of good local products, and nutritionally oriented. No foreign terms give false pretense to a good meal here.

"The guest rooms, with splendid views of the undulating Ponderosa timber stands, are replete with the feel of the thirties. The

bathrooms are Crane at its very best: circa 1935. The housekeeping
is exemplary."                                        —*Dr. F. M. Hinkhouse*

Open mid-June through Labor Day.
23 rooms, 14 cottages, all with private bath.
Rates $37–$42.
No credit cards.
Public coffee shop, dining room, and lounge.
Manager: Ed Edwards.

*—————————————————————————Portland*

## The Mallory Hotel
729 S.W. 15th Street
Portland, Oregon 97205
Telephone (503) 223-6311

"The Mallory is an old, well-maintained bargain hotel just a few
blocks from the city's main shopping mall. It is replete with funky
stairways, mail chutes, and a pleasant dining room just off the main
lobby."                                               —*Margaret Zeigler*

"A wonderful hotel—clean, bright, cheerful, and with an unusually
courteous staff. The food was not in the top range, but it was a
marvelous value at the price."                       —*Miranda Mackintosh*

Open all year.
144 rooms, 135 with private bath.
Rates $25–$50.
Credit cards: American Express, MasterCard, Visa.
Public dining room and bar.
Manager: Linda J. Anderson.

## The Westin Benson
309 Southwest Broadway, at Oak Street
Portland, Oregon 97205
Telephone (503) 228-9611

"Perhaps there are at best a dozen hotels in America that can be
considered great. Certainly the Westin Benson would be among the
top contenders for such a rating. Like other great but intimate
hotels—the Connaught in London, the Sacher in Vienna, and the
Lancaster in Paris—the Benson is handsome in the grand manner.

Its lobby suggests a drawing room more than a registration area. The menu in the London Grill is rich and varied, as is the selection from the wine cellar. Over eight decades, the Benson has had but a half-dozen general managers. Such a pattern palpably affects the quality of service. The traditional sense of American hospitality is alive and well in the heart of a great American city."

—*Dr. F. M. Hinkhouse*

Open all year.
330 rooms, all with private bath.
Rates $62–$110. Weekend packages $54.96 per night, single or double, including parking and a split of champagne.
Credit cards: American Express, MasterCard, Visa.
Manager: Paul Himmelman.

# Sunriver

**Sunriver Lodge**
Sunriver, Oregon 97701
Telephone (503) 593-1246 or toll-free (800) 547-3922; toll-free in Oregon (800) 452-6874

"A friend who vacations regularly at the lodge puts it well: 'I enjoy outdoor sports, the fine arts, creature comforts, and the quiet, relaxed life of Oregon's High Desert country. The annual Sunriver music festival attracts people from all over the American West, most of whom I like and enjoy seeing. Likewise, when I want to ski, Mount Bachelor is nearby. Its snow is in mint condition, as is the lodge's kitchen.'

"I agree with her completely."        —*Dr. F. M. Hinkhouse*

Open all year.
350 rooms, all with private bath.
Rates $50–$90 for rooms, $113–$158 for private cottages.
Credit cards: American Express, Carte Blanche, Diners Club, MasterCard, Visa.
Manager: Bud Gavino.

# Wolf Creek

**Wolf Creek Tavern**
P.O. Box 97
Wolf Creek, Oregon 97497
Telephone (503) 866-2474

# OREGON 91

"Wolf Creek is not even a town—just a country store/post office, gas station, and this wonderful inn. Acquired by the Oregon State Parks and Recreation division in 1975, it reveals long-forgotten crafts and portrays the evolution of a roadside inn."

—*Paul and Al Verta Williamson*

"The tavern is an imposing structure of Douglas fir built in Classical Revival style and painted white. One legend is that it was built by Chinese laborers, brothers under the skin of those who were to build the transcontinental railroads—or so it was introduced to me by an American scientist of Cantonese descent. Whatever its origins, however, it is a classic stagecoach stop from America's golden age; its rooms are thoroughly dated from the Oregon Territory. Built to serve passengers between Portland and Sacramento, the tavern has remained in continuous operation. Hospitality in front of the inn's roaring fire has been offered to such diverse guests as President Rutherford B. Hayes, Jack London, Sinclair Lewis, and Clark Gable.

"There were some sixty stagecoach stops along this route, according to Vernon Wiard, the innkeeper, who will regale you with stories about their journeys. In taverns, inns, and posthouses, passengers could get food and drink and a night's rest in a room with a parlor, if you had enough gold dust; in the top-floor dormitory if you did not. The dormitory served on special occasions as a ballroom for an elegant event for the ranchers, farmers, miners, and businesspeople who were carving out fortunes in the verdant Rogue River Valley of southern Oregon."     —*Dr. F. M. Hinkhouse*

Open all year.
8 rooms, all with private bath.
Rates $19–$29.
Credit cards: MasterCard, Visa.
Restaurant with wine and beer license.
River rafting, hiking, and gold-panning nearby.
Greyhound bus service.
Innkeepers: Vernon and Donna Wiard.

_____ *Yachats*

**The Adobe Inn**
P.O. Box 219
Yachats, Oregon 97498
Telephone (503) 547-3141

"Its name continues to perplex me: what has adobe got to do with this landscape? The inn is situated directly in front of and only slightly above the waves of the Pacific. Its architect utilized the pure theater of the scene to its fullest. The rooms are large, as are the windows. A well-placed fireplace dominates many of them. From a capacious chair it is wonderful to watch the surf, whipped by the ever-present west wind, crashing against the rocks and driftwood that combine to make the Oregon coast so magnificent. Spray, worthy of an impressionistic Turner canvas, is sent high into the air, dampening the flight of a sea gull.

"Day begins here in the drum-shaped dining room with a breakfast of razor clams and eggs, or the house omelet, larded with black caviar from the sturgeon of the nearby Columbia River. In between that and lunch, walk along the tidal pools and enjoy the light bouncing off the damp rocks or the solitary cry of a gull skating toward the dark forests behind the inn."          —*Dr. F. M. Hinkhouse*

Open all year.
Rates from $22 without ocean view, from $39 with view.
Credit cards: MasterCard, Visa.
Greyhound buses serve Yachats.
Manager: George Staats.

Do you know a hotel in your state that we have overlooked? Write *now*.

# _South Dakota_

## Custer

**State Game Lodge**
Highway 16A
Custer State Park
Custer, South Dakota 57730
Telephone (605) 255-4541

The lodge, near all points of interest in the Black Hills area, is set in the midst of one of the largest state parks in the country. There are lakes and streams, and herds of buffalo, deer, elk, and mountain goats. The menu reflects the setting: pheasant and buffalo are specialties of the house. The rooms are divided between the original lodge and a newer motel annex.

"This is one of my special favorites. The Game Lodge hosted President Coolidge in 1927 and President Eisenhower in 1953."
—_George McGovern_

Open about May 10 to October 1.
47 rooms, 20 cabins, all with private bath.
Rates $32–$55 lodge and motel, $32–$53 cabins.
No credit cards.

Public bar and restaurant.
Innkeepers: Jim and Mary Jo Hegert.

_____*Hill City*

**Sylvan Lake Resort**
Custer State Park (Box 1000)
Hill City, South Dakota 57745
Telephone (605) 574-2561

Around the original stone-and-wood lodge in the northwest corner of Custer State Park a resort complex has grown up that includes a number of cabins, a café, and a general store. The focus of the activity here is Sylvan Lake itself, with its fishing and paddle-boating opportunities.

"The lodge on top of the hill is built of golden limestone and large logs. Beyond its broad halls are large rooms, providing comfortable quarters for visitors. The dining room, which reflects the culture of the Dakota Indians, provides high-quality food. The chef is justly proud of his variations on the theme of the American steer. Vegetarians would be pleased by the wide range of other dishes offered as entrées or side dishes. The lodge is proud of its own farm." —*Dr. F. M. Hinkhouse*

Open May through September.
29 rooms, 21 with private bath; 13 cabins; 22 housekeeping cottages.
Rates $35–$55. Special rates off-season and for family reunions and special parties.
Credit cards: American Express, MasterCard, Visa.
Public bar and restaurant.
Innkeeper: Arthur W. Janklow.

Rates quoted were the latest available. But they may not reflect unexpected increases or local and state taxes. Be sure to verify when you book.

# _Washington_

## Cathlamet

**Cathlamet Hotel**
67–69 Main Street
Cathlamet, Washington 98612
Telephone (206) 795-8751

"This sleepy little lumbering and fishing town on the banks of the Columbia River boasts both an interesting hotel and restaurant—Pierre's, right next door to the Cathlamet Hotel. Both are owned by Pierre Pype, a former Chicago businessman who fell in love with the town and decided to put his expertise and efforts into making a super eatery and hostelry here. Eat only at Pierre's: the other establishments in town cannot be recommended. The hotel is done in 1920s style, with Art Deco stained glass in the small upstairs lobby. Most of the rooms have sinks, but do not have private baths; very clean baths are available down the hall. The rooms are small but comfortable."
—_Margaret Zeigler_

Open all year.
12 rooms, 2 with private bath.
Rate $28.50, including continental breakfast.

Credit cards: MasterCard, Visa.
Innkeepers: Pierre and Claire Pype.

_____ *Coupeville*

## The Captain Whidbey Inn
2072 West Whidbey Island Inn Road
Coupeville, Washington 98239
Telephone (206) 678-4097

"Years ago, when the summer's heat got out of hand in Arizona (where I was founding director of the Phoenix Art Museum), I would flee to Seattle and sail on to the magical islands a ferry's ride away. In that way, I discovered the Captain Whidbey Inn on a heavily forested isle discovered by Captain Vancouver. In that sylvan retreat I found splendid isolation, sunny-crisp weather, and the century-old, two-story inn hewn from madrona logs. My hosts, the Stephen Stone family, then, as now, provided superb hospitality, spacious rooms, and good food and drink. The inn's library, dominating the second floor, has a collection of first editions and current international magazines.

"The inn, with its own dock on Penn Cove, used to berth ships from Seattle, Tacoma, Vancouver, and Victoria. The Captain Whidbey can offer guests local oysters, Dungeness crab, delicate baby lamb, or properly aged beef. The dining room, like the Chart Room bar and the common room with its fieldstone and beachstone fireplace, has paintings reflecting on the beauty of land and sea by Dennis Argent, whom I call the inn's artist in residence."

—*Dr. F. M. Hinkhouse*

Open all year.
29 rooms and cottages, 20 with private bath.
Rates $30–$67.50, including continental breakfast.
Credit cards: MasterCard, Visa.
Public bar and restaurant.
Innkeepers: John and Jeff Stone.

Details of special features offered by an inn or hotel vary according to information supplied by the hotels themselves. The absence here of a recreational amenity, a bar, or a restaurant doesn't necessarily mean one of these doesn't exist. Ask the innkeeper when booking your room.

# Eastsound—Orcas Island

**Beach Haven Resort**
Route 1 (Box 12)
Orcas Island
Eastsound, Washington 98245
Telephone (206) 376-2288

"This delightful resort on one of the few inhabited islands in the San Juan chain is accessible to the mainland by the ferry from Anacortes. We found Beach Haven the most rustic yet well furnished and maintained place on the island. We spent a week resting, reading, hiking, boating, and canoeing. The accommodations range from one- to three-bedroom cabins to one- or two-bedroom deluxe apartments. All have fully equipped kitchens, some have fireplaces. They are strung out among the pines along the shore—and the sunsets are breathtaking.

"The small town of Eastsound, the metropolis of the island, has a supermarket, which makes shopping easy. There is a laundry at the airport. A number of good restaurants—among them Bilbo's and the Chambered Nautilus—make dining out a pleasure."

—*Margaret Ziegler*

Open all year.
12 cabins, 3 houses, 3 apartments.
Rates $45–$119.
No credit cards.
No restaurant or bar.
Ferry service to island by Washington State Ferries. Telephone (206) 464-6400 or toll-free outside Seattle area (800) 542-0810.
Innkeepers: Steve and Shirley Dalquist.

**Outlook Inn**
Main Street (Box 210)
Eastsound, Washington 98245
Telephone (206) 376-2581

"The slowing down begins on the hour-long ferryboat ride from Anacortes. There is the expanse of sky and water, jeweled by wooded islands and distant snowcapped mountains. Disembarking at the tiny port of Orcas, one drives through several miles of rolling meadows and primitive forests to the quaint village of Eastsound and the end of East Sound Bay. The inn is across the street from the driftwooded beach; the window boxes are full of flowers, and the large windows along the front are bordered with the etched designs of another day. Within, the little lobby has soft red wallpaper, antique wood, copper, and houseplants. A small chapel, an interdenominational gathering place, was built of wood from one of Washington State's oldest farmhouses. The inn is owned by the Louis Foundation, whose head, Louis (just Louis), can frequently be found reading, painting, or preparing a Sunday 'contemplation.'

"The inn's food is famous on the island, always cooked to order. During the growing season salad makings come from the vegetable garden and fresh herbs from the garden or greenhouse. Fish are caught and served the same day. There are herb teas, homemade soups, homemade breads and pies, and about twenty wines in stock.

"The bedrooms are homey and, above all, colorful. Some of the beds and bureaus are antiques. Rooms have adjustable wall heaters and washstands with hot and cold running water, but the bathrooms are those of an old hotel—off the hall, but within easy reach of rooms. The front bedrooms look out to the sound with its fadeaway borders of steep blue hills. The back bedrooms look out over the pond and the gardened hillside.

"There are many activities on the island: tennis, indoor and outdoor swimming, fishing, boating, and some horseback riding. The island is an excellent place for bicycling. Hikers or drivers can take a trip through Moran State Park, with its lakes and waterfall, up Mount Constitution to the old stone tower for a bird's-eye view of the San Juan islands, the floating snowclad range of the mainland, and right below, the lakes. Orcas is an inspiring place for painters and photographers. Easy trips by ferry or chartered plane or boat can be made to other islands. Jacques Cousteau brings his boat into these waters because the scuba diving can be excellent. Others rejoice in the varieties of birds that nest on Orcas or migrate through, in the deer, and in the unusual flowers. Interestingly enough, there are no poisonous plants on the island, no poisonous mushrooms, no harmful animals—nothing that will hurt man."

—*Darthea Stalnaker*

Open all year.
30 rooms, 3 suites, 13 with private bath.
Rates $29–$60.
Credit cards: MasterCard, Visa.
Turn-of-the-century public bar, home-style cooking in dining room.
Innkeeper: John Beithan.

Turn to the back of this book for pages inviting *your* comments.

---

**Rosario Resort**
Eastsound, Washington 98245
Telephone (206) 376-2222 or toll-free in Washington
State (800) 562-8820

"Back in 1905, Robert Moran, mayor of Seattle, hankering for a
retreat from urban life, built a handsome, Mediterranean-style villa
on Orcas Island. The home was stately and gracious, and when a
visiting royal came to the Northwest—such as Queen Marie of Ru-
mania—Rosario was a port of call on the itinerary. Moran's mansion
lodge is the center of today's activities, providing elegant rooms—
ask if you want to stay there and not in newer accommodation. The
music room, then as now, is dominated by Moran's 26-rank pipe
organ.

"The surrounding farmland, donated to the State of Washington,
became Moran State Park. It is overlooked by the dramatic slopes
of Mount Constitution. At the mountain's feet are four sylvan
lakes."                                               —*Dr. F. M. Hinkhouse*

Open all year.
216 rooms and suites, 209 with private bath.
Rates $45–$175.
Credit cards: American Express, Diners Club, MasterCard, Visa.
Public bar and dining room.
French, German, Italian, Swedish, and Vietnamese spoken.
Resident Manager: Gary Vaughn.

---

## *Langley*

**Whidbey House**
106 First Street(P.O. Box 156)
Langley, Washington 98260
Telephone (206) 221-7115

Langley is on South Whidbey Island in Puget Sound. From this
new-old inn, there are views of Saratoga Passage, Camano Island,
and the North Cascade Mountains. The island is reached by ferry
from Seattle.

"The innkeeper, Priscilla Golas, has traveled the world as a flight
attendant, and she knows what a guest needs to feel comfortable.
This is a small bed-and-breakfast inn of three rooms, each decorated with lovely old antiques and fabrics with wallpaper to match.

Priscilla delivers a basket of hot homemade muffins with coffee to the rooms every morning. She is hoping to open a restaurant in 1984."
                                                        —*Leslie Rose*

Open all year, except January.
3 rooms, all with private bath, private entrance, and deck.
Rate $55, including continental breakfast.
Credit cards: MasterCard, Visa.
Reached by Washington State Ferry.
Innkeepers: Priscilla Golas and Arthur Bauer.

_____*Packwood*

**The Packwood Hotel**
P.O. Box 256
Packwood, Washington 98361
Telephone (206) 494-5431

The Packwood Hotel, on the route between Mount St. Helens and Mount Rainier, is a 75-year-old building made entirely of cedar. The present owners, who are restoring it, have kept much of its original furniture, including a huge old-fashioned bathtub that is a favorite of guests.

"Teddy Roosevelt was supposed to have stayed in this wonderful hotel, which has been bought by a couple from California who are fixing it up. There is an old woodburning stove in the Victorian sitting room downstairs, and a big dog who lies around in front of it. There is a gingerbready front porch all the way around, with petunias hanging off it. The color scheme was not particularly spiffy when we were there, tending to electric blue. And there were some weird rules on the door of our room, but that didn't bother us."
                                                        —*Martha Miles*

Open all year.
9 rooms, 2 with private bath; 4 cabins.
Rates $20–$24.
Credit cards: MasterCard, Visa.
No restaurant, but there are 2 across the street.
Innkeepers: Michael and Linda McGrath.

If you would like to amend, update, or disagree with any entry, write *now.*

_Port Townsend_

## James House
1238 Washington Street
Port Townsend, Washington 98368
Telephone (206) 385-1238

"This restored Victorian house was built in 1891, at a time when Port Townsend, on the northeastern tip of the Olympic Peninsula, expected to become the New York of the West Coast, and to have the terminus of the transcontinental railroad. Neither of these things came to be, and the town withered away, being restored and revamped only in the last quarter century. A breathtaking array of Victorian houses stands on a tall bluff above the harbor and the commercial parts of town. James House commands a view out to sea.

"We had the garden suite: two rooms in the brick-walled basement with ground-level windows (we even had a view). The suite was full of antiques, including brass beds, and there were bowls of fresh-scented rose petals in every room. There was a woodburning stove, which we used one damp, chilly evening. Outside our suite there was a game room, with bookshelves of reading material. We ate our breakfast in the inn's kitchen with other guests, enjoying homemade breads (three different kinds each morning) and homemade jellies and jams."                                    —_Margaret Ziegler_

Open all year.
12 rooms and suites, 4 with private bath; 1 cottage.
Rates $40–$80, including continental breakfast.
Credit cards: MasterCard, Visa.
No public bar or restaurant.
Bus service from Seattle via Greyhound and Jefferson Transit.
Innkeeper: Deborah La Montagne.

## Manresa Castle
Seventh and Sheridan (P.O. Box 564)
Port Townsend, Washington 98368
Telephone (206) 385-5750

"Port Townsend is a town of about 5,000 people, a sort of arty community with antique stores and galleries. There are people living here in retirement and younger people coming to escape California and find a more relaxing life.

"This castle atop a hill with walls of solid brick two feet thick is an attractive place that the owners, the Smith family, are continually upgrading. The castle was once a Jesuit retreat; some of the stained-glass decoration came from the old chapel. The Smiths have done all the renovation work themselves. The posts with the gas lamps along the driveway were built of old bricks from the wall that once ran in front of the grounds. Inside there are 50 to 100 paintings, and antiques in all the rooms. Personal service is maintained here, although business grows every year."   —*Jerry Tennant*

"The castle offers a good view, but we had a second-rate room. In fact, above the first floor, the inn is not charming. The place was shabby (orange shag carpets) and inhospitable. The employees were surly and unhelpful."   —*Vernon Brown and Wendy Stewart*

Open all year.
36 rooms, all with private bath.
Rates $51–$75.
Credit cards: American Express, MasterCard, Visa.
Public restaurant and bar.
Innkeepers: Mr. and Mrs. Ronald Smith.

---

**Quimper Inn**
1306 Franklin
Port Townsend, Washington 98368
Telephone (206) 385-1086

"Absolutely faithful Victorian atmosphere—even some metal bathtubs and tubs with gargoyle feet! The hosts are young, happy people, anxious to offer the finest in personal attention. Naturally, homemade breads, croissants, jellies, and cakes are provided at breakfast."   —*Peter Stone*

"My visit was my introduction to the Olympic Peninsula and the Pacific Northwest. It was wonderful!"   —*Joanne Hill*

Open all year.
6 rooms, 2 with full bath, 2 with half-bath.
Rates $45–$60, including breakfast.
No credit cards.
No bar or restaurant.
Italian and Spanish spoken.
Innkeepers: Mariii Lockwood and Paoli Wein.

# *Quinault*

## Lake Quinault Lodge
South Shore Road (P.O. Box 7)
Quinault, Washington 98575
Telephone (206) 288-2571

Lake Quinault Lodge, in the Olympic National Forest, was built as a log hotel in 1896, destroyed by fire in 1923, and rebuilt in 1926 by a Seattle printer, Frank McNeil, with the backing of a local lumberman named Ralph Emerson. The Northwest's top craftsmen came to work on the comfortable and spacious lodge. Over the years, the hotel has expanded, but without the destruction of its 1920s core.

"The lodge, at the southern end of the rain forest and Lake Quinault, looks much older than it is. I was overcome by the setting. (The food was great, too.) Franklin Roosevelt visited the place in 1938 and was so charmed that he named the area a national forest."
—*Myrl Aldrich*

Open all year.
54 rooms, 46 with private bath.
Rates $40–$75 double.
Credit cards: MasterCard, Visa.
Public restaurant and bar.
Two buses daily from Aberdeen.
Innkeepers: Larry and Marge Lesley.

# *Seattle*

## The College Inn
4000 University Way N.E.
Seattle, Washington 98105
Telephone (206) 633-4441

"While at the University of Washington, I discovered the inn in desperation when I had to send a visitor somewhere and nothing else was available. I liked it very much and consequently sent quite a number of people there. The difference between this hotel and all the others in the area is the College Inn's totally personalized service. You are completely at home there. The essence of the hotel is really European, and I am very prone to European hotels. It is similar to a hotel in London that I frequent a lot. Innkeeper Gladys Fred has furnished the hotel through estate sales: there are magnificent brasses, lovely old beds—a style that I could describe as comfortably spartan, with nothing too fancy and everything in excellent taste. The fourth-floor lounge/breakfast room has a superb piano. The antiques are local, and chosen to restore the character that the turn-of-the-century hotel had to begin with. Gladys Fred has put her own personality into all of this. She is a warm, accepting sort of person, and so a broad range of people are comfortable there."

*—Thomas Hutchinson*

Open all year.
27 rooms, all with sinks and sharing baths.
Rates $25–$45, including continental breakfast.
Credit cards: American Express, MasterCard, Visa.
No restaurant.
Innkeeper: Gladys L. Fred.

---

## Four Seasons Olympic Hotel
Fourth and Seneca
Seattle, Washington 98111
Telephone (206) 621-1700

"I chose the Olympic because of a recommendation in an earlier edition of this book, and found that the hotel had reopened after extensive renovations by the Four Seasons. It surpassed our expectations. Everything had been done to make hotel living a pleasurable experience, from the well-trained staff to the elegant and comfortable decor to the beautifully presented and delicious food. Thick terry-cloth robes were provided for guests to enjoy the pool, sauna, and exercise room. The concierge was helpful in making arrangements for us, shoes were polished at night, pressing was provided in an hour, and room service was prompt. In this age of convenience it was a pleasure to be pampered by people who seemed to enjoy doing it."

*—Grace Hudson*

Open all year.
451 rooms and suites, all with private bath.
Rates $95–165 single, $115–165 double.
Credit cards: American Express, Carte Blanche, Diners Club, MasterClub, Visa.
Reservations Manager: Colleen Merrow.

All inkeepers appreciate reservations in advance; some require them.

_____ *White Salmon*

## The Inn of the White Salmon
P.O. Box 1446
White Salmon, Washington 98672
Telephone (509) 493-2335

Loretta and Bill Hopper, the innkeepers, have been working for five years on the restoration of this 1937 house with a view of the Columbia River and Mount Hood. Mr. Hopper is a commercial pilot who knows what kind of hotel he is tired of, so he has added many extra touches to this small hotel to make the service personal. Meanwhile, Mrs. Hopper is becoming famous around the Northwest for her stupendous breakfasts: any number of interesting egg dishes, several dozen kinds of home-baked pastry, and a variety of fruit dishes are all in her repertoire.

"We travel around the state a great deal looking for out-of-the-way places. This is the best we have found. I have never had such a perfect weekend."                                             —*Sally Egan*

Open all year.
19 rooms, all with private bath.
Rates $33–$56, including full breakfast.
Credit cards: American Express, MasterCard, Visa.
Innkeepers: Loretta and Bill Hopper.

Would you be so kind as to share discoveries you may have of charming, well-run places to stay in Europe? Please write to *Europe's Wonderful Little Hotels and Inns,* c/o Congdon & Weed, 298 Fifth Avenue, New York, New York 10001. (By the way, a new and greatly expanded edition of this splendid guide is now available at your bookseller's.)

# _____ *Wyoming*

## Cody

**Irma Hotel**
1192 Sheridan Avenue
Cody, Wyoming 82414
Telephone (307) 587-4221

"The Irma Hotel was built by William F. Cody—better known as
Buffalo Bill—and opened on November 1, 1902. It was named for
his youngest daughter. During this period he was traveling far afield
with his Wild West Show, and he liked to return to this small town
and stay in his suite at the Irma or at his ranch on the South Fork
of the Shoshone River.

"Many of the bedrooms at the Irma have been renovated and
named after people associated with Cody, such as Frank Blackburn,
the sheriff; Vern Spencer, a guide and trapper; and Caroline Lock-
hart, novelist and journalist. The dining room has been enlarged,
a private dining room added, and the floors carpeted. The cherrywood backbar, presented to Buffalo Bill by Queen Victoria, was
made in France, shipped to New York, and taken by rail to Montana,
then by horse-drawn freight wagon to Cody. The old metal ceiling
showed several bullet holes where some overexuberant cowboy had

shot into the air, narrowly missing people in the bedrooms above. The innkeeper has replaced the old ceiling with a new one, which is almost an exact replica of the old.

"Many festive occasions have been held at the Irma, such as the annual Trappers' Ball and the Stampede Ball—affairs which have unfortunately been discontinued. Wallace Reid, of silent-movie days, was a desk clerk here long before his rise to stardom. The hotel, which is on the National Register of Historic Places, is in the heart of the downtown business district on an avenue named after Buffalo Bill's good friend, General Sheridan. Cody is a tourist town only fifty miles from the eastern entrance of Yellowstone Park. Attractions include the Cody Stampede, held in July, and the Buffalo Bill Historic Center, known for its Western art."

*—Margaret Martin*

Open all year.
41 rooms, all with private bath.
Rates $30–$60.
Credit cards: American Express, MasterCard, Visa.
Public bar and restaurant.
Manager: Douglas R. Greenway.

_____*Evanston*

**Pine Gables Inn**
1049 Center Street
Evanston, Wyoming 82930
Telephone (307) 789-2069

"We recommend this remarkable place, which offers the comfort of Grandma's home within easy walking distance of Evanston's shopping district. It is furnished with lovely oak antiques, some of which can be bought. There is an antiques shop on the premises, where browsing is fun. The inn is nicely decorated, and the owners are never too busy to chat with guests." *—Ilene and Jim Silver*

Open all year.
6 rooms, 2 with private bath.
Rates from $28.50, including continental breakfast.
Credit cards: Diners Club, MasterCard, Visa.
2 blocks to bus depot; 3 blocks to Amtrak station.
Innkeepers: Jessie and Arthur Monroe.

Do you know a hotel in your state that we have overlooked? Write *now*.

_Saratoga_

**Hotel Wolf**
101 East Bridge Street (P.O. Box 1298)
Saratoga, Wyoming 82331
Telephone (307) 326-5525

The Hotel Wolf, built in 1893, served for some time as a stagecoach stop. Early in this century, it became the center of fishing expeditions—at one point taking on the new name of Sisson's Hotel, for Baldy Sisson, a trout fisherman who drowned in the North Platte River.

"The hotel really is old in feeling; there's plumbing that dates back a bit. But there has been a real attempt here to restore the old hotel, with its high ceilings and nice veranda. The dining room is large and charming and overwhelmingly accommodating." —*Odette Baehler*

Open all year.
17 rooms, 6 with private bath.
Rate $24 double, with bath.
Credit cards: MasterCard, Visa.
Public bar and restaurant.
Innkeepers: Doug and Kathy Campbell.

_Sinclair_

**The Parco Inn**
Sinclair, Wyoming 82334
Telephone (307) 324-6658

The history of the settlement of Parco, six miles from Rawlins, was unique in the every-man-for-himself West. Its founder was the oil-man Frank Kistler, a visionary who wanted the workers at his refinery to have the best a planned community could offer. In 1923 and 1924 he built them houses and shops; he brought in a symphony orchestra and founded a baseball team. And he built a hotel designed by a leading Denver architectural firm, Fisher and Fisher. It was no ordinary small-town tavern, but a grand hotel with a ballroom, barbershop, and recreation facilities, and it became the heart of the community. Before the 1960s brought the motel to the West, the Parco Inn was the stopping place of the glamorous set: Amelia Earhart, Howard Hughes, and Robert Taylor were among its well-known guests. Big bands filled the ballroom with wonderful sounds. Then came a slump. But now Parco and its hotel are being restored by a history-conscious town. The old settlement has become a historic district, and the inn has an enthusiastic new innkeeper.

"Parco Inn is located high on the sagebrush plain of south central Wyoming, next to a refinery. What makes it worthy of inclusion in this book? It is an oasis. It has history. It has charm. It is roomy. From the Civil War cannons in the front to the red tile roof with its Spanish-style towers, to the spacious lobby, the Parco is different. The Union Pacific Railroad, built by Colonel Dodge and the Casement brothers—and swindled by the Credit Mobilier—passes just across the plaza.

"I first stayed at the inn, then the Sinclair Hotel, before the election of 1958, and watched election ads in black and white on the TV set in the lobby. A room for a struggling young traveler was then $3.25. Truck drivers got a discount.

"This is a place to relax. There is no spectacular scenery. No movies. No tourist traps. The food is wholesome mid-America. The inn is being restored by Rick Mentink, son of an old Wyoming line. This is worth a stop or stay."                    —*Paul M. Buchanan*

Open all year.
55 rooms and suites, 45 with private bath.
Rates $18.50–$38.50.
No credit cards.
Bar and restaurant.
Innkeeper: Rick Mentink.

American hotels and inns generally list rates by the room, assuming one person in a single, two in a double. Extra people in rooms normally incur extra charges. Where rates are quoted per person per day, at least one meal is probably included under a Modified American plan (MAP). A full American Plan (AP) would include three meals.

# Part Three

## Southwest and South Central

*Arkansas*

*Colorado*

*Kansas*

*New Mexico*

*Oklahoma*

*Texas*

# _Arkansas_

## Eureka Springs

**Crescent Hotel**
Prospect Street
Eureka Springs, Arkansas 72632
Telephone (501) 253-9766

"The description of Eureka Springs as the 'little Switzerland of America' is a grotesque one. This town is very different, and can stand quite comfortably on its own American merits. It is a town of steep streets that wind up and down the hillside, of Victorian shops and ornate houses. It is a town that has become a meeting place for musicians, artists, and writers. The two places to stay here are the massive Crescent, perched high on a hill, or the small New Orleans, tucked away in a curve of the main street. Both are exceptional: your choice depends on your mood.

"You sweep up to the front entrance of the Crescent as you would arrive at a Victorian country home. The lobby has a stone fireplace and a period reception desk. The Crystal dining room is cavernous and has a handsome wood floor, a grand piano and, unfortunately, an ugly glass centerpiece that is tempting to bump into 'accidentally.' There is a pub on the lower level, and from the Top of the

Crescent lounge you can sit in a wicker chair, nurse your aperitif, and look out over the valley. The rooms have all been restored: lots of footstools, lamps, and marble-toppled tables.

"The hotel had its grand opening in 1886 and was used exclusively by grand people known as the carriage set. A period followed in which it was a summer resort and a junior college for women the rest of the year. Then for an unhappy three years in the 1930s it was a hospital for the 'curing of cancer'—the operator was later charged with fraudulent practices. Now it is back in business as a hotel, owned by a Kansas City company.

"The town is full of surprises. For the religious there is the giant Christ of the Ozarks, a model Holy Land, and the Passion Play, performed from May through October. For the less religious or irreligious there is Silver Dollar City, a kind of Ozark Disneyland (which has a fine crafts festival in the autumn). If you are lucky, you can also find some memorable music in local taverns."

—*David Wigg*

Open all year, except January 5–March 1.
76 rooms, all with private bath.
Rates $40–$110.
Credit cards: American Express, MasterCard, Visa.
Innkeeper: Jerry Hope.

---

**Dairy Hollow House**
P.O. Box 221
Eureka Springs, Arkansas 72632
Telephone (501) 253-7444

"Three people whose own life stories have fairytale aspects created Dairy Hollow House out of a derelict farm of 1880s vintage. It was just across the dirt road from the house where one of its three owners, Crescent Dragonwagon, an itinerant writer with a hippie bent, had put down roots some years before. Bill Haymes, a traveling folk musician met Crescent while singing in Eureka, and their friendship led to her dedicating her first novel to him, and to this business venture. Ned Shanks, the third member of the trio, is a preservation and restoration expert who met Crescent in a historic house in Little Rock. Their friendship lasted into marriage, and they now live in Atlanta.

"A maximum of four people can stay at Dairy Hollow. The Rose Room, with roses on the wall, deep rose trim, rose-colored sheets and towels, and a Dutch rose quilt, has a double brass bed. The Iris Room, ditto on the iris theme and color scheme, has twin iron beds. There is a common living area, or parlor, connected to the kitchen.

"Breakfast at Dairy Hollow House is already legend. It is prepared by one of the dairymaids, whose footsteps on the porch are the first sound you hear in the morning besides the singing birds and a distant rooster. Dressed in a red-checked peasant skirt, the dairymaid puts a paper at your door, offers you tea or coffee in bed, then sets about creating breakfast. Ours was a German pancake, baked on a hot iron skillet, filled with fruit and topped with butter, lemon juice, and powdered sugar—served after the fresh-squeezed orange juice served in frosted champagne glasses.

"Dairy Hollow House is in the woods, but only five minutes by car or a fifteen-minute walk from downtown."          —*Starr Mitchell*

Open all year.
2 rooms, both with private bath.
Rates $45 single, $49 double, Sunday–Thursday; $55 single, $59 double, Friday and Saturday, including breakfast.
No credit cards.
Innkeepers: Jan and Blake Brown.

---

# New Orleans Hotel
63 Spring Street
Eureka Springs, Arkansas 72632
Telephone (501) 253-8630

'Eureka Springs must be one of the oddest towns in America. Its architectural oddities alone have earned it at least seven mentions in the old 'Ripley's Believe It or Not' column. It blossomed late in the last century from wilderness to a city of 16,000 when a local judge cured a crippling leg infection by bathing in its springwaters. World War I medical advances cut the bottom out of the curative water business, and Eureka Springs, like many spa towns, shrank to one-tenth its previous size. But the architecture of a Victorian hill town—if you can imagine such a thing—remained intact. Tourists returned in the mid 1960s, mostly busloads of fundamentalist Christians come to witness the new Sacred Projects established just outside town by Gerald L. K. Smith, a largely forgotten evangelist now, but one of America's leading preachers of the 1930s. Smith's pilgrims brought others in their wake. In the seventies, the old Victorian shops of Spring Street blossomed into workshops and salesrooms for a more-than-unusually-talented cluster of artists and craftspeople.

"Phil Schloss is one of the town's interesting newcomers. He took over the old New Orleans Hotel—so called thanks to two rather spartan cast-iron balconies along the facade—and restored the place, not to splendor but to something resembling its original shabby gentility. How nice to see someone restoring a hotel that was never really first class, and being true to its history. There are impromptu musical evenings in the high-ceilinged lobby, hearty soups in the ground-floor dining room, and sixteen hamburger variations in the cozy basement pub called The Quarter.

"A fascinating little hotel in a fascinating corner of America. You'll never come to Eureka Springs by chance. But if you're within 100 miles, it's worth a detour."        —*Mechtild Hoppenrath and Charles Oberdorf*

Open all year.
22 rooms and parlor suites, all with private bath.
Rates $36–$50.
No credit cards.
2 restaurants with cocktail lounges.
Trailways bus service. Air connections at Harrison or Fayetteville.
Innkeepers: Philip and Florence Schloss.

Rates quoted were the latest available. But they may not reflect unexpected increases or local and state taxes. Be sure to verify when you book.

*Historic Redstone Inn,*
*Redstone*

# Colorado

## Aspen

### Hotel Jerome
330 East Main Street
Aspen, Colorado 81611
Telephone (303) 925-1040

"Downtown Aspen, the mecca of snowbirds and musicians, is dominated by a handsome landmark built during the peak of the silver-
mining era. The Jerome, opened in 1889 and renovated in 1949,
provides rooms from simple singles to suites with spacious parlors.
No two rooms are alike; each has a distinct personality. Throughout
the hotel's brick structure there is a patina of faded elegance. Attractions of the Jerome include its bar, restaurant, shops, and a disco
called the Rock'n Horse."                —*Dr. F. M. Hinkhouse*

Open all year.
35 rooms, all with private bath.
Rates $34–$50 single, $46–$60 double.
Credit cards: American Express, MasterCard, Visa.
Taxi service from Aspen airport.
Manager: Dan Baxter.

_____*Boulder*

**Hotel Boulderado**
2115 13th Street
P.O. Box 319
Boulder, Colorado 80306
Telephone (303) 442-4344

Boulder, the home of the University of Colorado with its Tuscan-style architecture, has long been one of the state's most pleasant and interesting cities. In additon to its fine climate and superb location, literally at the base of the Rockies, the city has benefited from a population with a strong sense of civic awareness. It was the people of Boulder who, at the turn of the century, raised the money to build a fine hotel that would reflect their pride in the town. The Boulderado opened with a crowd of 2,000 in attendance on New Year's Eve 1908. There have been slumps—and several changes of ownership—since, but the hotel has survived as an important turn-of-the-century landmark. The present owners, who took over in 1980, have been engaged in extensive restoration and redecoration.

"One can only hope that what happened to the Hotel Boulderado will happen to many other fine old hotels in America. In its worst days, the hotel had sunk to flophouse level, according to one of its previous managers. But now the Victorian mezzanine lounge has been restored, and the magnificent glass ceiling and cherrywood stairs and banisters of the lobby have been saved. At last, the mood of America is one of preservation and restoration. The Boulderado reflects it well."                                      —*David Wigg*

"The Boulderado is fun to look at, inside and out, and it has life and spirit. A perfect place it is not. There are cigarette machines in the beautiful lobby, piped music (but sometimes it's chamber music), and a clientele that, at least on one hot July day, acknowledged no dress code. But once you get above the lobby and the mezzanine that looks down on it (a good place to have a drink), the hotel regains its dignity. The halls are wide, the rooms large and cheerfully appointed, the service (mainly by collegians) willing. The attractive restaurant, Winstons, yielded a dinner and a breakfast that were only passable. There is also an Italian restaurant, not visited. For runners, the foothills of the Rockies are just a few blocks away. All things considered, the Boulderado is a colorful, pleasant old place, to which I'd happily return."                        —*Tom Congdon*

Open all year.
42 rooms and suites, all with private bath.

Rates $45–$120.
Credit cards: American Express, Carte Blanche, Diners Club, MasterCard, Visa.
2 restaurants, 3 lounges, and an oyster bar.
French, German, and Spanish spoken.
Innkeeper: Steve Adams.

---

## Briar Rose
2151 Arapahoe
Boulder, Colorado 80302
Telephone (303) 442-3007

"In Boulder you have a pleasant choice. You can stay at the atmospheric old period piece, the Boulderado, which is a hotel. Or you can stay at the Briar Rose, which is a two-story house, with extensions, in a suburban neighborhood. Attractive from the outside but nothing special, it fools you with its modesty. Within is a woman named Emily Hunter, tall and with a soft Virginia accent, who will show you to one of eleven very pretty rooms. On the door of each is a wreath of grapevine and pink ribbon. The decor tends to soft pink and dusty rose, and the rooms are homey and light. There are old prints on the walls and, on the bureaus and tables, roses and potpourris provided by a neighbor, a 100-year-old Englishwoman who specializes in such embellishments. The Rose Room is a favorite with honeymooners, for its pink, semicircular fan headboard—popular even though you have to go downstairs for a bath. You return to your room at night to find mints or chocolate truffles on your pillow—and perhaps to discover that Emily Hunter has straightened up your room and hung up your strewn clothing, just to be nice.

"But the reasons for staying at the Briar Rose go beyond mere decor and the personal touch. Ms. Hunter turns out to be a most intelligent person with interesting friends, who drop by some Sundays to attend the so-called Briar Rose Tea and Chamber Music Society—poetry readings and musical performances and good conversation. One friend, Richard Schwartz, runs an old bookstore; he has 65,000 books on sale and gives away 700 a day, his overstock, from bins on the sidewalk. Ken Kesey stayed at the Briar Rose for ten days, when he came to the Jack Kerouac conference in Boulder, and there are all sorts of people who are in town to visit the University of Colorado or the new liberal arts college called the Naropa Institute. Not that any of this intellectuality is in any way imposed on you; you can bypass it with ease and just sit back at breakfast and enjoy the croissants brought fresh to the house each morning. But if you're educated and in the mood, staying at the Briar Rose can be a very agreeable experience."    —*Tom Congdon*

"To say the least, it is probably the most wonderful place in the state."    —*Rick Madden*

Open all year.
11 rooms, 6 with private bath.
Rates $49 single, $65 double, including breakfast.
Credit cards: American Express, MasterCard, Visa.
No restaurant, but small suppers can be prepared for guests.
Innkeeper: Emily Hunter.

## *Central City*

**The Golden Rose Hotel**
102 Main Street
Central City, Colorado 80427
Telephone: (303) 582-5060

"Central City is a nineteenth-century gold rush mining town less than an hour west of Denver. As you approach it through spectacular mountain gorges, you see people panning for gold along the creek, trying their luck. And suddenly, in a steep valley, there is Central City, a Victorian town (rebuilt after a fire in 1874) in a near-perfect state of preservation. At ground level there is tourist stuff, but there are rows of marvelous facades—including that of an opera house built by the gold miners for their own delight and still delighting Coloradans with its perfect acoustics.

"Just down Main Street from the opera is the Golden Rose Hotel. Newly restored by John Feinberg and Harold Pyle and their wives, it is a treat and a treasure. All the rooms are decorated in nineteenth-century antique furnishings—no reproductions—and recast Victorian lighting fixtures. The wallpapers are hand-printed from designs of William Morris and Christopher Dresser, and the embossed paper called Supaglypta is used as wainscoting in the halls. The bathrooms, which have radiant heat panels, are of marble, porcelain, and old brass; the wooden toilet seats are themselves antiques.

"The attention to detail has been great, both here and in the adjacent building that houses a lively Western bar, two extremely handsome restaurants, and more guest rooms. There are shortcomings—the unshaded lamps shine too brightly, and without the moderating effect of Victorian bric-a-brac the dark, heavy furniture can be a bit too imposing. But these are quibbles. The Golden Rose is a wonderful place, and the food, more or less *nouvelle cuisine,* is of high quality. One could stay for days without noting all the perfect touches, the ingenious harmonies. The hotel even has a file telling which of its beds are hard, soft, or extra long—the better to meet its guests' preferences.

"Central City is a good home base for skiing (cross-country and downhill) and excursions into the Rockies. The opening of the opera season in early July is supergala, and the Central City Jazz Festival (third weekend in August) is another kind of terrific. But the Golden Rose is, in itself, worth the trip. It has to be one of the best new-old hotels in the country."                              —*Tom Congdon*

Open all year.
26 rooms, 23 with private bath.
Rates $35–$100.
Credit cards: American Express, MasterCard, Visa.
2 restaurants and a bar.
Innkeepers: John Feinberg and Harold Pyle.

## Clark

**The Home Ranch**
P.O. Box 822K
Clark, Colorado 80428
Telephone (303) 879-1780

The Clark Ranch is on the Elk River, eighteen miles north of Steamboat Springs and near the Routt National Forest and the Mount Zirkel wilderness area. The owners, who had been involved in summertime dude ranching in Wyoming, opened the ranch in 1978 as a year-round operation. There is skiing in the winter and fishing and llama trekking in warmer weather.

"While in Colorado I found an incredibly beautiful ranch, with a two-story log lodge with common rooms, a library, a grand piano, a sunshiny family-style dining room, and a bar. The log cabins, nestled in aspen woods, have exposed beams. Each has two bedrooms, two baths, and a lovely living room with woodburning stove and coffeemaker. On the front porch is a hot tub. I realize that this isn't a 'little hotel or inn,' but the very special charm and warmth found in the hotels in this book can also be found at the Home Ranch."                              —*Susan Bachrach*

Open all year.
5 cabins, all with private bath.
Rates from $92 per person per day, double occupancy; $585 per person per week, AP, including skiing and horseback-riding lessons. Two-night minimum stay.
No credit cards.
Guests met at Steamboat Springs airport.
Innkeepers: Ken and Sharon Jones.

# Colorado Springs

## The Hearthstone Inn
506 North Cascade
Colorado Springs, Colorado 80903
Telephone (303) 473-4413

"Within the past few years, the Hearthstone has expanded from one to two 1865–1866 Victorian houses. They are furnished in antiques of the period, including musical instruments such as an organ and piano that guests may play. In the dining room, there is an ample supply of coffee and tea, and guests may come in for a cup anytime. The large living room is a perfect place to sit and relax, read a good book, or listen to music. With the room comes a delightful family-style breakfast in the larger of the two dining areas. There is always a delicious main course with fresh spice breads and fruit juice.

"Pike's Peak can be seen from the inn. Just a few minutes away are the Pro Rodeo Hall of Champions, the Flying W Ranch (and supper club), Manitou Springs, art museums, shopping areas, and the downtown attractions. A number one place."
—*Sondra Lee Davidson; also recommended by M. S. Wyeth, Jr.*

Open all year.
15 rooms, 13 with private bath.
Rates $48–$75, including full breakfast.
Credit cards: MasterCard, Visa.
Airport at Colorado Springs. Trailways and Greyhound service.
Innkeepers: Dorothy Williams and Ruth Williams.

# Denver

## The Brown Palace
321 17th Street
Denver, Colorado 80202
Telephone (303) 825-3111

"This is Denver's answer to the Plaza in New York. Or, more likely, it is what the Plaza would like to be. Anyone who knows the Brown Palace will try to get a room in the old wing. The new wing, known as the Tower, is motel-ish. There is an interior court and a stained-glass ceiling in the lobby, which rises nine floors. (An American flag hangs from the seventh to the fourth floor.) In the heart of the downtown district, the hotel, which opened in 1892, dates back to the time when visitors arrived by Pullman."          —*Jack Goodman*

"A superb old hotel."                                    —*Dr. F. M. Hinkhouse*

"This is not a cozy little hotel, by any means. The vast rotunda by itself prevents intimacy, as do the numbers of people bustling through. The Brown Palace is a big commercial establishment. But it has great period charm."                         —*Tom Congdon*

Open all year.
476 rooms and suites, all with private bath.
Rates $80–$450.
Credit cards: American Express, Carte Blanche, Diners Club, Mas-
    terCard, Visa.
General Manager: William Sweet.

---

**The Oxford**
1600 Seventeenth Street
Denver, Colorado 80202
Telephone: (303) 628-5400

"If I ran Denver's Brown Palace Hotel, I'd worry about the Oxford, once a badly deteriorated old hotel near Union Station, at the other end of downtown, now beautifully restored and made into a really first-rate establishment.

"The lobby is furnished like a venerable men's club, complete with an immense Oriental carpet and a vast fireplace that works. The halls are unusually wide and lined with good antiques. Every room is decorated individually and, from what I could see, well; each has at least a few old pieces, and twelve rooms feature French Art Deco pieces. The sheets are 100 percent cotton, the pillows are down (foam is available). There is a plant in every room—a living thing! —and there are magazines on hand such as *Town & Country* and *Business Week.* On your pillow at night is a mint and a card saying: 'Some gentle dreams/The hours of sleep beguile.' Shoes left outside the door are shined—magnificently—by morn, free. The staff is highly professional and agreeable. In short, you get the feeling that the hotel spares no effort or expense to do things right.

"I wasn't able to take meals there but wish I could have. The Oxford Club is a large, handsome, paneled dining room; when they restored it they discovered that the grimy old chandeliers were made of sterling silver. The Sage Room is less pricey, with hardwood floors, bentwood chairs, white linen, and a good view of Union Station and brick facades across the street. The Cruise Room is an Art Deco bar—silver furnishings with flamingo lighting; an experience.

"The Oxford is quite a place. It reaches a very high standard."
—*Tom Congdon*

Open all year.
82 rooms, 70 with queen-size beds, 12 with twin beds.
Rates from $85.
Credit cards: American Express, Diner's Club, Carte Blanche, MasterCard, Visa.
2 restaurants, a bar, and a lounge.
General Manager: Robert BanBergen.

*Durango*

## The General Palmer House
567 Main Avenue
Durango, Colorado 81301
Telephone (303) 247-4747

The General Palmer House, one of Colorado's oldest continuously operating hotels, is the centerpiece of a restoration project known as Rio Grande Land. The old Western-style, right-on-the-sidewalk cowtown hotel named for the founder of the Denver and Rio Grande Railway, has been restored to its Victorian incarnation, with shining brass and colorful glass lighting. From Durango, visitors can take a narrow-gauge railway trip to the historic mining community of Silverton.

"This hotel is centrally located for visitors to the Mesa Verde cliff dwellings, the San Juan Mountains, and the Purgatory ski area."
—*C. R. Ellsworth*

Open all year.
35 rooms, all with private bath.
Rates $40–$68.
Credit cards: American Express, Carte Blanche, Diners Club, MasterCard, Visa.

Public restaurant and bar.
Airport limousine service.
Innkeeper: Carolyn Warner.

---

## Strater Hotel
699 Main Avenue (P.O. Drawer E)
Durango, Colorado 81301
Telephone (303) 247-4431

"The Strater, a Durango landmark, has been privately owned since 1882. It is like a second home to me; I still manage to get there three or four times a year. There are two very fine restaurants in the Strater: the Columbian Room and the Opera House, our favorite. In the summer, guests are entertained by singers from the hotel's theater. After dinner, or a theater performance, you need not leave the hotel for further entertainment: just step through the lobby to the Diamond Belle Saloon. Visitors and local people gather here to enjoy a drink, the honky-tonk piano, and the singing, all in a Gay Nineties atmosphere."                     —*Alberta Word*

"Every room pleases: dining rooms, saloon, theater, lobbies, and shops—but best of all are the bedrooms. The whole place is furnished in genuine Victoriana, no two rooms alike. It's like visiting the home of a fabled grandmother who has maintained myriad family treasures in mint condition—plus laid on impeccable plumbing, unobtrusive individual thermostats, and three-way light bulbs that actually work three ways.
"This is the place to headquarter while you explore the Four Corners marvels, which range from the San Juan alpine wilderness to the Navajo desert. Or you can visit the local cattle auction. One caution: try the Strater at least slightly out of season. They tend to bring in busloads of tour groups in season."           —*Betty Feazel*

Open all year.
94 rooms, all with private bath.
Rates $42–$60.
Credit cards: American Express, Carte Blanche, Diners Club, MasterCard, Visa.
Public bar and restaurants.
Manager: Tim Bridwell.

Where are the good little hotels in Boston? Philadelphia? Omaha? Dallas? If you have found one, don't keep it a secret. Write *now*.

_____*Empire*

## The Peck House
83 Sunny Avenue (P.O. Box 428)
Empire, Colorado 80438
Telephone (303) 569-9870

The Peck House, Colorado's oldest continuously operating hotel, was built as a mountain home in 1860 that took in visitors from the East who had come to prospect or invest in the booming West. James Peck and his family had come west from Chicago for the same reasons as their guests: the Pecks struck it lucky, and rich, on gold. The original four-room house soon grew to include a second story, a long veranda, and an aspenwood pipeline that delivered fresh water to the home from a spring. The Peck House has never ceased to be a social center for the town of Empire.

"The windows of the parlor, bar, dining room, and sitting room all look out over the lush green valley of Empire and the creek bed where the Ute Indians camped on their way over the Berthoud Pass to the Winter Park and Middle Park hunting grounds. One can hike from here through Union Pass, south of Empire, and pass trout lakes and the homes of some of the area's older families, as well as the scars of the mining activity that made Empire a gold camp in the nineteenth century." —*Odette Baehler*

"I arrived with a small rush of anticipation. The hotel, with its fine view, had a tattered Western look that was appealing, even endearing. But no one was on hand to receive me, and when someone did show up the welcome was muted, to say the least. The room I was shown was a bit dingy, and the public rooms were done up in undistinguished bric-a-brac—more nearly tacky than quaint. I didn't stay. But it struck me that the Peck House might be a good choice for a family with kids. Probably not a bad place if you approach it in the right frame of mind. Its plain, slightly run-down style might commend it if one has had a surfeit of hyperrestoration." —*Tom Congdon*

Open all year.
10 rooms, 5 with private bath.
Rates $30–$70.
Credit cards: American Express, Carte Blanche, Diners Club, MasterCard, Visa.
Public bar and restaurant.
Spanish spoken.
Bus service from Denver.
Innkeepers: Gary and Sally St. Clair.

———————————————————————— *Georgetown*

## The Neighbors

Georgetown/Baehler Resort Services
Box 247
Georgetown, Colorado 80444
Telephone (303) 569-2665

The historic silver-mining town of Georgetown, about an hour's drive west of Denver, is a veritable museum of Victorian and neo-Gothic structures that have remained intact thanks to a miraculously disaster-free history and the relentless watchfulness of a local population aware of the importance of what they have. Unfortunately the town's wealth of preserved and restored buildings did not include a hotel, and travelers who wished to spend the night were forced to make do with motel-style accommodations. In the last couple of years, Odette Baehler, who was a regular inn-goer and local tourism promoter, has made an effort to fill the gap by organizing an accommodation service based on Georgetown's historic homes. Guests can rent restored and completely equipped houses by the weekend, week, or month. Odette, while not strictly an innkeeper, says she does "mother hen" her guests, taking them on a short tour of the town and providing them with literally a basketful of advice on the area's attractions and restaurants. One of the houses in her collection is called The Neighbors.

"Within easy walking distance of Georgetown's famous Silver Queen restaurant, The Neighbors is a charming Victorian home where my mother, daughter, niece, and I recently spent a vacation. We were delighted with the three-bedroom house, and spent much of our time doing needlepoint in the white wicker furniture in front of the fire. It was a sentimental journey for us: my mother remembered vacationing in Georgetown when she was a child. We are glad that some things don't change." —*Carol S. Werner*

Open all year.
12 houses.
Rates from $100 a day, depending on size of house.
No credit cards.
Mother Hen: Odette Baehler.

Turn to the back of this book for pages inviting *your* comments.

## _Glenwood Springs_

**Hotel Colorado**
526 Pine Street
Glenwood Springs, Colorado 81601
Telephone (303) 945-6511 or toll-free in metro Denver
623-3400

"With towers modeled after the Villa di Medici, the hotel has dominated the town since 1893. Ages ago, the Indians refreshed themselves in the hot mineral vapor caves nearby, where today's visitor can still take the air. But it was the hotel that brought royalty to the springs, the waters of which were captured in the world's largest outdoor hot pool. Teddy Roosevelt made the Hotel Colorado his Western White House in the spring hunt season, and it was here that the teddy bear is thought to have originated.

"Today the hotel retains its grandeur, with fine stonework and halls wide enough for two overfed, overdressed couples to promenade with room to spare. Alas, decor and service fell on hard times in the 1970s. But the hotel is being returned to its original elegance by Sam Wisdom, who earned a fine reputation restoring the Eureka Springs Hotel and Kansas City's Muehlebach. Amazingly, some of the Colorado's original chandeliers were found stored in an unused stairwell: it turns out that utter neglect can be the best preserver, next to loving care."                                    —*George Herzog*

Open all year.
106 rooms, 22 suites, all with private bath.
Rates $42–$175.
Credit cards: American Express, Carte Blanche, Diners Club, MasterCard, Visa.
Public bar and restaurant.
Continental Trailways and Amtrak train service.
Innkeeper: Matthew Young.

## _Ouray_

**House of Yesteryears**
516 Oak Street (Box 440)
Ouray, Colorado 81427
Telephone (303) 325-4277

Ouray, a city 7,800 feet above sea level and completely surrounded by peaks of the San Juan Mountains, was a favorite camping place for Ute Indians, who bathed in the curative springs in the valley floor. The river that flows through here is named Uncompahgre, from the Ute word for hot springs. The area around Ouray, once booming mining country, is now devoted largely to cattle, horses, and sheep. From here, visitors can travel easily to the mining towns of Telluride, Rico, and Animas Forks. Mesa Verde with its Indian cliff dwellings is also within reach, as are the towns of Durango and Silverton.

"The House of Yesteryears, a family-run guesthouse, fills the need for something different for your vacation. The antiques are of interest to the whole family. Ray's homemade muffins and coffee are a good start to the day, and sitting on the porch with a view over Ouray is a nice way to end it. The place is small, and room rates are reasonable, so booking in advance is a must."   —*Doug Sanford*

Open June 10 to September 10.
8 rooms, 2 with private bath. Breakfast served to guests for $1; no other meals.
Rates $20–$40.
No credit cards.
Innkeeper: Raymond C. O'Brien.

———————————————————————*Redstone*

**Historic Redstone Inn**
0082 Redstone Boulevard
Redstone, Colorado 81623
Telephone (303) 963-2526

John Cleveland Osgood was a coal baron, industrialist, financier, and the business partner of such powerful men as J. P. Morgan and John D. Rockefeller. His cousin was Grover Cleveland, the twenty-second (and twenty-fourth) president of the United States. In this mining village of Redstone, Osgood built himself a manor house he called Cleveholm, chalets for married miners, and the Redstone Inn for bachelor employees and guests. The inn, opened in 1902, had a barbershop, laundry, telephone, steam heat, and electric lights—nothing could have been more up to date. The inn has recently been completely renovated.

"The drive from Denver to Redstone is through spectacular scenery all the way—through the Eisenhower tunnel to Dillon and Vail, along the Colorado River through Glenwood Canyon, along the Roaring Fork River to Carbondale, then eighteen miles south along the Crystal River to Redstone. Only ten miles farther south is Marble, now a ghost town but once the place where high-grade Colorado marble was quarried from 1907 to 1941. The Redstone Inn is real Colorado. There are no strangers here, and you don't feel you are hitting the tourist trail."          —*Harriet Morgan*

"My friend and I shared a two-double-bed room that was light and airy. I had the best night's sleep I'd had in a long time, with the windows wide open to a cool breeze and the soothing sound of the Crystal River outside."          —*Jeanne C. Lee*

Open all year.
24 rooms, all with private bath.
Rates $25–$40.
Credit cards: MasterCard, Visa.
Spanish spoken.
Manager: Roger Wiegener.

## *Telluride*

**New Sheridan Hotel**
231 West Colorado Avenue (Box 980)
Telluride, Colorado 81435
Telephone (303) 728-4258

"Telluride is a skiing area in a box canyon completely surrounded by mountains that rise from the valley floor. You can walk to the ski lift from your hotel. The town is also well known for its annual Labor Day weekend film festival, which is held at the New Sheridan complex. From time to time the valley is also full of good music. The New Sheridan, a restored Victorian hotel, is right on the main street, near some awfully nice shops and restaurants."     —*Odette Baehler*

Open all year.
30 rooms, 9 with private bath.
Rates $30–$66.
Credit cards: American Express, MasterCard, Visa.
Public restaurant and bar.
Spanish spoken.
Limousine service to Montrose airport; nearest bus at Ridgeway.
Manager: Susan Paasehe.

If you would like to amend, update, or disagree with any entry, write *now*.

# Kansas

## Harper

**Rosalea's Hotel**
121 West Main Street (Box 121)
Harper, Kansas 67058
No telephone

"This must be America's most eccentric hotel—in the nicest sense of the word. You even have to be a 'member' to get a room: Rosalea will send you an evening's supply of reading material on her place and its place in rural Kansas, which you will have to consult just to figure out how to book a room. Rosalea, an artist with a sixties view of life and a renegade from a Mennonite farming community, bought the old Patterson House Hotel in 1968 for $1,500. The house happened to be between the homes of Carry Nation and Susanna Salter: Rosalea describes the setting as 'three places of women's accomplishment.' An artist, Rosalea painted her hotel red, made part of it an art gallery featuring her work and the work of friends and former guests (real artists can sometimes trade an art-work for a room), named her inn the Oasis of the Bible Belt, and promptly earned the suspicion and opposition of the townsfolk, whom Rosalea depicts on one of her brochures as Neanderthal specimens.

"Rosalea is quite specific on what kind of people like her hotel: 'mavericks, freethinkers, and rugged individualists.' She won't let anyone see a room in advance. She won't let people who are not guests wander into the place—in fact she has just opened a restaurant across the street called the Tourist Trap and she recommends that gawkers sit there and watch her from a safe distance.

"What are the rooms really like? I stayed in one covered with tinfoil with a montage on the ceiling of pictures of Richard Nixon, John Kennedy, Pope John XXIII, and civil rights leaders. A tailor's dummy in one corner modeled a belt and scarf created by Rosalea and a sign complaining that no one had bought it, so it had been relegated to the Upstairs Permanent Collection. 'How our stupid society loves to see artists struggle and suffer,' it says. The room, with a platform bed, was surprisingly comfortable. There were two cane chairs from the Methodist church, a fan, a radio that wouldn't turn off until unplugged, a warm bathroom with a handsome tub and sculpture on the walls.

"Much of the ground floor is a huge lobby, with a long wooden table, artwork on the walls, many books, and a box of 'Nice Objects to Handle.' The office was called, not surprisingly, the Disaster Area."
—*David Wigg*

Open May 1 to October 31.
10 rooms, 4 with private bath.
Rates $16–$36.
No credit cards.
Innkeeper: Rosalea.

All inkeepers appreciate reservations in advance; some require them.

*Sagebrush Inn,
Taos*

# New Mexico

## Pecos

**Broken Drum Ranch**
Route 2 (Box 100)
Pecos, New Mexico 87552
Telephone (505) 757-6194

Within the last year, the guest ranch known as Tres Lagunas has been taken over by new owners, the Veit family. Gay Veit says they intend to continue operating the ranch pretty much as it has been run for many years. While we wait for travelers to report on the new management, here is a comment from a longtime visitor to the ranch.

"We have spent some time each summer for over thirty years at this rustic yet beautiful ranch with three lakes at an elevation of 7,500 feet in the Sangre de Cristo Mountains. The Pecos River provides the focal point for this relaxing spot, less than an hour from historic Santa Fe. Guests have plenty of choices for their activities: nature, reading, fishing, horseback riding, hiking, shopping, or even opera-going in Santa Fe. The food and maid service are excellent."

*—Fred Zimmerman III*

Open all year.
13 cabins.
Rates $50–$60 per person, AP.
Credit cards: Master Card, Visa.
Innkeepers: The Veit family.

_____*Santa Fe*

**Hotel de Vargas**
210 Don Gaspar Avenue
Santa Fe, New Mexico 87501
Telephone (505) 983-3391

Santa Fe, in the Sangre de Cristo Mountains, is a resort area all year round, with skiing in winter and a wide range of summer outdoor activities. The city and its architecture owe much to their Indian and Spanish history. Adobe building is kept alive, as are the crafts that flourished here.

"For the budget conscious, the de Vargas offers a quaint old place in not-perfect repair that attracts many nice people in their twenties and thirties."
                                                            —*George Herzog*

Open all year.
87 rooms, 43 with private bath.
Rates $20–$26.
Credit cards: American Express, MasterCard, Visa.
Spanish spoken.
Greyhound and Trailways buses to station ½ block away.
Innkeeper: Mrs. Pat Vigil.

_____

**The Inn at Loretto**
211 Old Santa Fe Trail
Santa Fe, New Mexico 87501
Telephone (505) 988-5531

"The classic adobe style of the hotel is consistent inside and out. The Plaza, heart of old Santa Fe, is only a block away, as are many of the best shops and museums. The rooms are appointed simply but comfortably. There is adequate parking, but you walk most places in Santa Fe."
                                                            —*Harry Kennedy, Jr.*

"The Inn is an amazingly successful blend of modern comfort and the adobe style." —*George Herzog*

Open all year.
139 rooms, all with private bath.
Rates $80–$98.
Credit cards: American Express, Carte Blanche, Diners Club, MasterCard, Visa.
Spanish spoken.
Shuttle to Albuquerque airport.
Manager: John F. Sexton.

---

## La Fonda
100 East San Francisco Street
Santa Fe, New Mexico 87501
Telephone (505) 982-5511

"La Fonda—the inn at the end of the Santa Fe Trail—makes much of its past. In the old hotel that stood on this site in the nineteenth century, Captain Stephen Watts Kearney celebrated his conquest of New Mexico for the United States, General H. H. Sibley was quartered when the Confederates took the city in 1862, General and Mrs. Ulysses S. Grant danced at a grand ball in 1880, and no less a figure than Billy the Kid washed dishes in the kitchen. That building was demolished in 1919, and the present soft-cornered, pueblo-style hotel took its place. It dominates the surprisingly modest plaza —nothing grandiose here to compare with the plazas of Mexican cities—a reflection of Santa Fe's role as a minor northern outpost of the Mexican Empire.

"La Fonda is the city's meeting place. Its large tiled lobby is ideal for sitting to talk or watch. The bedrooms are traditional New Mexican, which means fine wooden furniture.

"Outside on the Plaza, walk slowly in the clean, thin air of the 6,999-foot altitude. In front of you is a slice of New Mexican history: the Palace of Governors, built in 1610, and the open-air market where Indians sell jewelry and leather goods. There are many restaurants within walking distance, gentle places with good jazz, soft-spoken waitresses, and satisfying if not adventurous food. The whole atmosphere of Santa Fe is that: tranquil and accepting."
—*David Wigg*

"La Fonda offers the most seasoned flavor of the Old West. La Plazuela, its grand, two-story courtyard dining room has good Mexican and continental dishes." —*George Herzog*

Open all year.
170 rooms, all with private bath.
Rates $64–$70 single, $74–$80 double, $125–$225 suites.
Credit cards: American Express, Carte Blanche, Diners Club, MasterCard, Visa.
Limousine service to Albuquerque airport.
Innkeeper: Eddie Smithson.

## Taos

### Hotel La Fonda de Taos
P.O. Box 1447
Taos, New Mexico 87571
Telephone (505) 758-2211

"The literary industry surrounding the work and life of D. H. Lawrence may be getting a little out of hand, and literary pilgrimages can be a bit phony. But during his gypsy life, Lawrence did spend time in some spectacular places, and this is one of them. After he died in Europe in 1930, his wife, Frieda, had his ashes brought here to be placed in a tiny building a few yards from their ranch house. Frieda was later buried under a stone slab a few paces to one side. The home, now owned by the University of New Mexico, was deserted when I arrived—just a few friendly donkeys ambling about. The view alone is worth the short climb: an avenue of pine trees slopes down the hill to the long, long stretch across the valley floor and on to the distant, snowcapped mountains. The visitors' book at Lawrence's grave is interesting to glance through. The pilgrims, inspired perhaps by the clear air, quote his poems or lapse into their own versions of Lawrentian free verse.

"The ranch is a few miles north of the tiny town of Taos, with its adobe buildings. On one side of its minute plaza is the La Fonda, with its fine, high-ceilinged lobby and walls covered with art, tapestries, and photographs. The manager has a few of Lawrence's erotic paintings that, unbelievably now, caused so much official outrage when they were exhibited in London in the 1920s. The paintings are not very good and, frankly, not very erotic. There are also photographs in the office of some of the many literary personalities who made their way at one time or another through this part of New Mexico.

"La Fonda's bedrooms are smallish, neat, and agreeably simple. You can eat at one of the restaurants nearby—one has a veranda overlooking the plaza, where local artists and dropouts, along with more conservative types, meet during happy hour. There is an Indian pueblo on the outskirts of town, and a Kit Carson museum full of bric-a-brac."   *—David Wigg*

Open all year.
24 rooms, 23 with private bath.
Rates $43–$86.
Credit cards: MasterCard, Visa.
Greek and Spanish spoken.
Manager: Saki Karavas.

---

**Sagebrush Inn**
South Santa Fe Road (P.O. Box 1566)
Taos, New Mexico 87571
Telephone (505) 758-2254

"Right away a person knows if he or she likes Taos and, if not, returns to some other larger city immediately. Taos has a definite personality; so does the Sagebrush Inn. The sacredness of private space is an unwritten code in Taos; however, if one chooses to become involved, the people are friendly and open. A wealth of talent lives in Taos: the actor Dennis Hopper, the writer John Nichols, and the painter R. C. Gorman, whose paintings are found in the dining rooms of the hotel.

"The Blair family have made many improvements and additions to the inn without spoiling the atmosphere; the decor of the newer rooms is the same as that in the older ones. There are several dining areas, one of which is covered with a skylight roof for year-round use. The walls in the lounge, offices, dining areas, and guest rooms abound with original art. To think of Taos is to think of the many galleries, the Talpa Hills, the Taos Mountains and the rich history of the Spanish, the Indians and the Anglos who have come and gone —or stayed—as time has passed."   *—Marilyn Foust*

"The one drawback here is the inn's position, right up against the highway. I thought it was basically a motel, cleverly and imaginatively disguised. The room I had was very ordinary and poorly furnished."   *—David Wigg*

Open all year.
63 rooms, all with private bath; 13 two-room suites, and 1 three-room, three-bath suite, with fireplaces.
Rates $38–$150.
Credit cards: American Express, Carte Blanche, Diners Club, MasterCard, Visa.
2 restaurants, and lounge with live entertainment.
French, German, and Spanish spoken.
Innkeepers: Ken and Louise Blair.

---

**The Taos Inn**
P.O. Drawer N
Taos, New Mexico 87571
Telephone (505) 758-2233

"Of all the places we have stayed in Taos, the Taos Inn is by far our favorite. There has been extensive restoration of this beautiful historic landmark, making it more comfortable without changing its old Southwestern style. The inn is within steps of the Taos plaza, and next door to the community auditorium, a center for the performing arts as well as galleries and craft shops. The inn is close to some good restaurants, like the Apple Tree, but the food at Doc Martin's in the hotel itself—seafood, Italian and Mexican dishes—is so good that a guest can happily stay within the inn for dining. Unlike most hotels in Taos, this inn also offers room service.

"Of the forty-one rooms, most have pueblo-style fireplaces, and each day in cool weather a supply of wood is left in your room. The fireplaces, part of the remodeling, were done by Carmen Velarde, an adobe artist-sculptor whose design has been featured by the National Folklife Festival at the Smithsonian Institution in Washington. Each fireplace was designed to complement its room; the rooms themselves differ from one another. But all rooms have the warm sense of a hacienda guest room, with lovely furnishings, antiques, and handwoven Zapotec Indian bedspreads. For those who care about such things, there is also color television, Jacuzzis, and a swimming pool at the inn.

"A special feature of the building is its two-story lobby with balconies and a sunken fireplace surrounded by *bancos,* also designed by Velarde. The lobby serves as a lounge area for the Adobe Bar, and is a favorite local gathering place for relaxing over a drink while listening to pleasant live music from the bar."

—*Susan and Art Bachrach*

Open all year.
41 rooms, all with private bath.
Rates $45–$75.
Credit cards: American Express, MasterCard, Visa.
Owner-managers: Feeny Lipscomb, Bruce Ross, and Scott Sanger.

American hotels and inns generally list rates by the room, assuming one person in a single, two in a double. Extra people in rooms normally incur extra charges. Where rates are quoted per person per day, at least one meal is probably included under a Modified American plan (MAP). A full American Plan (AP) would include three meals.

# Oklahoma

## Durant

**Bryan Hotel**
101 West Main Street
Durant, Oklahoma 74701
Telephone (405) 924-3796

The Bryan, built in 1928, was designed by Jewell Hicks, who also designed Oklahoma's state capitol. The hotel has had what they call a rich and varied history—meaning some of it was wild and improper—but that reputation faded with the revival of interest in the building's architecture and potential as a fine old city hotel. Since 1980, restoration under the direction of two Dallas businesspeople, Guy M. Wills and Ruth Mcleod, has revealed copper awnings, terrazzo floors with marble baseboards, and Bohemian glass chandeliers. The original Otis elevator still works.

"This historic hotel is in an area rich in Indian lore. The local historical society is continuing to search for and add items of history to the hotel. We were given a tour of the building, riding in the old elevator that is still in working order. Durant is near the Lake Texoma recreation area. In town, many small shops offer interesting shopping for visitors." —*Barbara E. Price and Kim Snyder*

Open all year.
40 rooms, 4 suites, all with private bath.
Rates $25–$30 single, $34–$40 double, $34–$50 suites.
Credit cards: American Express, MasterCard, Visa.
Coffee shop and supper club in hotel.
Guests met free at Eaker Field.
Manager: Cortland Mcleod.

## Oklahoma City

**Skirvin Plaza Hotel**
1 Park Avenue at Broadway
Oklahoma City, Oklahoma 73101
Telephone (405) 232-4411 or toll-free (800) 654-4500

Big Bill Skirvin, a local cattle and oil baron, got it in his head more
than half a century ago to build Oklahoma City the grandest hotel
the state had ever seen. The result was the Skirvin, full of beautifully
carved wood, brasswork, and chandeliers. The hotel has recently
been restored, symbolic of a revival of Oklahoma City itself.

"The hotel, now renovated, has always been one of the more elegant older hotels in the state. There is a huge lobby with high,
carved pillars, and an extraordinary, high-ceilinged dining room
with large windows. It is a lavish hotel with Southern-style warmth."
—*Judy Boswell*

Open all year.
200 rooms, 10 suites, all with private bath.
Rates $65–$350.
Credit cards: American Express, Carte Blanche, Diners Club, Mas-
terCard, Visa.
Restaurant and bar.
Spanish spoken.
General Manager: Coyne Edmison.

Where are the good little hotels in Boston? Philadelphia? Omaha?
Dallas? If you have found one, don't keep it a secret. Write *now.*

# _Texas_

## Austin

**The Driskill**
117 East 7th Street
Austin, Texas 78701
Telephone (512) 474-5911

"The atmosphere of the Driskill is half Beaux Arts splendor and half twenties club. A piano enlivens the lobby. Bellhops are available, attentive, and able to double as concierges. The guest rises in a wood-paneled elevator to a labyrinth of hallways with a scattering of antiques. My room was modest, but comfortable. If you want the best, ask for the L.B.J. Suite.

"The older part of the hotel is supported by stunning marble columns on two floors. A delightful oasis in this wing is the Cabaret, an intimate lounge of plush booths separated by etched-glass panels. Service here blends knowledge, formality, and friendliness. The paneled splendor of the formal dining room has now been restored, and the lobby lounge has been made more comfortable."

_—George Herzog_

"The story of the Driskill begins in 1886, when it was built by Colonel J. L. Driskill, a cattle baron who furnished beef to the

142

Confederate Army during the Civil War. The hotel was a pacesetter over the years. It was the first hotel south of St. Louis to have electricity; the first stagecoach in Texas ran from the Driskill to Houston; and the first long-distance phone call in Austin was placed at the hotel.

"The building is of modified Romanesque design, with lots of marble inside and an exterior of native Texas brick and limestone. Many of the old rooms have solid maple fireplace mantels that stretch to the ceiling; some are adorned with mirrors. Over the years the ballrooms have been the site of numerous inaugural balls for the governors of Texas—Austin is the state capital. During Lyndon Johnson's presidency, the hotel served as headquarters for the White House press corps on the president's visits to Texas. In 1964, the Johnson family awaited election results in the Jim Hogg suite.

"The hotel's Maximilian Room is one of the most elegant meeting and banquet rooms in the country. The room has eight panels fitted with gold-leaf mirrors, a wedding gift from Maximilian, Emperor of Mexico, to his bride, Carlotta. Atop each mirror is a gilt likeness of the Empress."                                          —*Ruth Fawcett*

Open all year.
185 rooms, 20 suites, all with private bath.
Rates $44–$94.
Credit cards: American Express, Carte Blanche, Diners Club, MasterCard, Visa.
Restaurant and bar.
French, German, Portuguese, and Spanish spoken. Sign language for the deaf.
Manager: Wanda L. Curry.

## Big Sandy

**Annie's Bed and Breakfast**
106 North Tyler (P.O. Box 928)
Big Sandy, Texas 75755
Telephone (214) 636-4307

"The inn is in the fourth turn-of-the-century home in this quiet East Texas town to be restored by the same owners. The first of their restorations, and the best known, is Annie's Tea Room. People come from miles around for lunch or dinner there. The atmosphere, country mixed with old Victorian grace, is special: the waitresses even dress in turn-of-the-century costumes. I mention the tearoom because that is where meals are served to guests of the inn, which is just across the street. Each of the inn's rooms has its own personality. All have antique furniture and some even have handmade quilts. The innkeepers, Tom and Rose Adams, are charming people, and Rose offers a special touch: she was born and raised in England.

"Big Sandy is a wonderful place for anyone wanting to escape city life and spend a day or two in the country. It is also a great stopover when traveling through the state. Two cities, Longview and Tyler, are nearby."                                                                    —*Lisa Roe*

Open all year.
14 rooms, 9 with private bath.
Rates $45–$100 double, including full breakfast; $104–$214 weekend for two persons, including packed picnic brunch Saturday and full breakfast in the Tea Room on Sunday.
Credit cards: MasterCard, Visa.
Innkeepers: Tom and Rose Adams.

# Castroville

## Landmark Inn
Castroville, Texas 78009
Telephone (512) 538-2133

Here is an inn in its own park, the Landmark Inn State Historical Site, run by the Texas Parks and Wildlife Service. The inn, with grounds that stretch to the Medina River, has a small museum in the building. There is also a gristmill on the site.

"This little inn, now part of a park, is over 100 years old. It should be listed."                                                                                      —*Mabel Suehs*

Open all year.
8 rooms, 4 with private bath.
Rates $13 single, $16 double.
No credit cards.
Innkeeper: Carolyn Scheffer.

# Dallas

## The Mansion on Turtle Creek
2821 Turtle Creek Boulevard
Dallas, Texas 75219
Telephone (214) 559-2100

"For those bold enough to venture west of the Hudson, only San Francisco and Dallas have the panache to carry off a distant version of '21'—and only Dallas would try. It more than succeeds: opulence is the culminating effect of all the detail. There is an adult breed of parking attendant who knows how to manage people, cars, and luggage unobtrusively. You step into a marbled reception hall where giant flowers, a glowing fire, and sheer space create a feeling that is at once grand and serene. Would you care to dine before seeing your room? The deskman arranges seating and freedom from luggage at a stroke. You enter the baronial splendor of Shepherd King's original mansion. A clubby bar done up with American paintings, a lounge for intimate conversations—these are merely passages to the great salon with its vaulted ceilings. Feast yourself on the signature dishes of '21.' Here, far from the rough side of Texas, both cuisine and conversation will pleasantly surprise you. Ready to retire? Half the rooms have the best view of the Dallas skyline. You've arrived at last. This one is magnificent!"

—*George Herzog*

Open all year.
143 rooms, 14 suites, all with private bath.
Rates $115–$180 single, $140–$205 double, $350–$650 suites.
Credit cards: American Express, Carte Blanche, MasterCard, Visa.
Restaurant and bar.
Arabic, Dutch, French, German, and Italian spoken.
Manager: Alexander de Toth.

---

## The Melrose
3015 Oak Lawn Avenue
Dallas, Texas 75219
Telephone (214) 521-5151

"Nearly all the other luxury hotels in Dallas are very large and/or very new. The Melrose was built in the early 1920s to last—with high ceilings, spacious public halls, huge windows, and lots of natural light. A reported $18 million was spent in 1982 to completely refurbish all the rooms, but the original tile floors in the huge bathrooms are intact, and so is the paneling in the library, a delightfully civilized room for cocktails. All the modern conveniences one wants are here, and all seem to work; the remodeling job was done with taste and a sense of scale. In a city dominated by the new, it

is pleasant to return to a quiet, traditional hotel. The dining room
was fine for lunch, but not recommended for a formal dinner."
—*Lee Simons*

Open all year.
185 rooms, all with private bath.
Rates $60–$120.
Credit cards: American Express, Carte Blanche, Diners Club, Mas-
terCard, Visa.
Restaurant and cocktail lounge.
General Manager: Charles Carroll.

**Stoneleigh Terrace**
2927 Maple Street
Dallas, Texas 75201
Telephone (214) 742-7111 or toll-free (800) 255-9299

"The Stoneleigh has both a bad and a good side. The most appealing feature of the hotel, to me, is its swimming pool: it is so soothing
to have a garden and greenery around while deep in the heart of the
city. The hotel's location is also convenient, and the breakfast prices
are most reasonable. But the hotel is a little on the run-down side,
and service was not up to par. By and large, though, the hotel tries
hard, and is friendly and pleasant."          —*Ursula Bender*

Open all year.
155 rooms, all with private bath.
Rates $50–$90.
Credit cards: American Express, Carte Blanche, Diners Club, Mas-
terCard, Visa.
Restaurant and bar.
Manager: C. J. Vannoy.

*Granbury*

**The Nutt House**
Town Square
Granbury, Texas 76048
Telephone (817) 573-5612

"One of the most charming hotels we have ever visited. Wonderful
home cooking. What it lacks in fancy it more than makes up for in

charm and good food. The hotel registry attests to how many people love it."                                        —*Mrs. Preston Nix*

Open all year.
7 rooms sharing bath; 1 apartment with private bath.
Rates $20–$30.
Credit card: MasterCard
Trailways buses serve Granbury.
Resident Manager: Madge Peters.

—————————————————————————*Jefferson*

## Excelsior House
211 West Austin Street
Jefferson, Texas 75657
Telephone (214) 665-2513

"The Excelsior House is, in my experience, one of America's unique and charming hotels. To me, the fascinating thing about it is the picture it presents of a bygone way of life. History fills every room. The Excelsior was built in the 1850s, with a wing added about twenty years later. In the old, open hotel register you can see the names of several presidents—Ulysses S. Grant, Rutherford B. Hayes, and my husband, Lyndon. It is said that Robert E. Lee was also a guest. The pages also bear the names of most of the famous players, minstrels, and drama groups that toured Texas in the early days. What exciting visions they conjure up! The furnishings speak of that period of American history. The old player piano came from Europe and was shipped up the Mississippi to the Red River and then the Bayou. In the 1870s, paddle steamers carrying both freight and passengers landed at Jefferson.

"A group of volunteers—the Jesse Allen Wise Garden Club—owns and operates the Excelsior. This remarkable group of women restored the old hotel to new life and usefulness, and what they have created is marvelously inviting. They laughingly say that with all of them having to decide jointly on wallpaper or resolving the problems of paying for the restoration, it was enough to give you hope that the United Nations itself might succeed."

                                        —*Mrs. Lyndon B. Johnson*

"Many guests use the Excelsior when attending Louisiana Downs horse racing from May through November. Therefore, reservations are at a premium Wednesdays through Sundays. We reserve rooms at least a year in advance. In addition to the Excelsior House, Jefferson has many antique shops, restaurants, museums, and restored homes. The best way to see the town is to take a surrey ride, with a Jefferson resident as driver and guide."

—*Walter and Anna Marie Osborn*

Open all year.
14 rooms, all with private bath.
Rates $23–$50.
No credit cards.
Bus service to Jefferson.
Innkeepers: The Jesse Allen Wise Garden Club.

---

## New Jefferson Inn
124 Austin Street
Jefferson, Texas 75657
Telephone (214) 665-2631

"Jefferson, in the beautiful pine forests of northeast Texas, is a lovely place in the spring and fall. Once a booming town, it is now quiet and peaceful. The citizens, who care about their heritage, have restored many of the homes in the downtown historic area. One thing that cannot be restored, however, is the river channel along which palatial steamboats sailed away to New Orleans. Many a bride and groom spent their honeymoon, as did my parents, aboard the old paddle-wheel boats on the way to plantations in Louisiana. The inn has the air of the late 1800s in East Texas, with its rooms furnished in the Victorian manner."

—*Mr. and Mrs. Kenneth Wickett*

Open all year.
22 rooms, all with private bath.
Rates $25 single, $30 double.
No credit cards.
Restaurant.
Innkeeper: George V. Delk; Manager: F. J. Fisher.

---

## Pride House
409 Broadway
Jefferson, Texas 75657
Telephone (214) 665-2675

"This is an 1890s Victorian mansion restored by Ray and Sandy Spalding and named for their son, Pride. The house is run by Sandy's mother, Ruthmary Jordan. The guest rooms are unique and splendidly designed. A 'dependency' at the rear of the house provides additional space. We were entertaining a large group when we stayed there, and were allowed to use the small parlor downstairs to gather for drinks with our friends before going to dinner downtown."                    —*Catherine and Bill Bailey Carter*

Open all year.
6 rooms and redesigned servants' quarters, all with private bath.
Rates $37.50–$60, including buffet breakfast.
Credit cards: MasterCard, Visa.
No restaurant or bar.
Innkeeper: Ruthmary Jordan.

_____*New Braunfels*

**Prince Solms Inn**
295 East San Antonio
New Braunfels, Texas 78130
Telephone (512) 625-9196

"Just thirty minutes northeast of San Antonio is the delightful German settlement of New Braunfels. The Prince Solms Inn, built in 1898, is just a block from the banks of the Comal River and a block from the town plaza with its old-fashioned gazebo. In the summer months, guests can frequently hear the sound of oompah bands. The inn's rooms are furnished with antiques, including canopy beds, bathtubs on feet, and solid oak dressers. Even the doorknobs are made of bronze. With 18-inch walls and ceilings 13 to 15 feet high, the hotel was obviously built to provide its guests with a cool respite from the hot Texas sun.

"Many of the hotel's features are historical items or details found in other locations and brought here to be reused and adapted. The 10-foot-high front doors with etched glass and the ceiling fans are from German-built homes in San Antonio's King William area. The limestone walkway outside the cellar dining room came from a county jail; part of the inscription is still visible."
                                        —*Ruth Fawcett*

Open all year.
11 rooms, all with private bath.
Rates $42–$100, including continental breakfast.
Credit cards: MasterCard, Visa.

2 blocks from Greyhound bus station.
Innkeeper: Ruth L. Wood.

## Rio Grande City

**La Borde House**
601 East Main Street
Rio Grande City, Texas 78582
Telephone (512) 487-5101

"Rio Grande City is a remote spot, far from the larger cities of
Texas, but an easy drive from the retirement centers of McAllen,
Harlingen, and others. The restaurant, which features border cuisine, is worth a stop during the long drive along the Rio Grande—
east or west. The hotel is a delightful oasis in the most unexpected
place." —*Lois Chiles*

Open all year.
8 historical rooms, 13 modern 1-room apartments, all with private
   bath.
Rates $55 for rooms, $40 for apartments.
Credit cards: American Express, MasterCard, Visa.
Bar and restaurant featuring border cuisine.
Innkeeper: Maria Luisa Sanchez.

## San Antonio

**La Mansion del Rio**
112 College Street
San Antonio, Texas 78205
Telephone (512) 225-2581; toll-free (800) 531-7208;
toll-free in Texas (800) 292-7300

"La Mansion lives up to the title of your publication. It is located
on the bank of the San Antonio River, along the River Walk (the
Paseo del Rio), within walking distance of everything. The hotel is
in a nineteenth-century building that was once a school begun by
the French brothers of the Society of Mary. Its rooms are tastefully
done and its food excellent." —*Mrs. W. J. Simmons*

Open all year.
350 rooms, 14 suites, all with private bath.
Rates $70–$97 single, $88–$115 double.
Credit cards: American Express, Carte Blanche, MasterCard, Visa.

2 restaurants and bar.
Spanish spoken.
Manager: James T. Boiles.

---

## The Menger Hotel
204 Alamo Plaza
San Antonio, Texas 78205
Telephone (512) 223-4361 or toll-free (800) 843-9999

"Next door to the Alamo, one of the oldest hotels in the region is still standing in its original form: the Menger. Built in 1859, it was originally intended to serve as a lodging for the numerous patrons of William Menger's brewery. But over the years, it became known as the finest hotel west of the Mississippi. Menger, a German brewmaster, migrated to Texas just eleven years after the fall of the Alamo and one year after Texas became a state. San Antonio was a Mexican town of 8,000 residents when Menger opened his brewery in 1855. In those days Indian raids were a constant threat. According to old newspaper clippings, the old bar at the Menger (a replica of the taproom at the House of Lords Club in London) was one of the most popular in the city—but unlike all the others, its patrons could not ride their ponies inside the saloon.

"The brewery has long since disappeared, but the bar, the hotel, and the tunnels underneath the structure remain. The hotel has expanded from an original 50 rooms to 300, including a new section. But the old section of the hotel and the bar still contain most of the original furnishings. In the King Suite you can find a 100-year-old gold-and-marble shaving stand left by onetime resident Richard King of the King Ranch. Canopy beds, elaborately carved mahogany chairs, and velvet sofas adorn the rooms, which open out onto the lobby with French-style wrought-iron balconies. For the antique lover, the only disappointments are the modern bathroom fixtures."                                                    —*Ruth Fawcett*

"At one time the Menger had alligators in its patio, but the amorous bull alligator's serenading kept the guests awake. So the alligators were donated to the zoo. The patio is still there—a beautiful subtropical garden with parrots and other birds. The hotel has quite a history. Teddy Roosevelt signed up volunteers for his Cuban campaign in the lobby and bar."                                    —*Henry A. Zepeda*

Open all year.
300 rooms and suites, all with private bath.

Rates $43–$55 single, $55–$67 double, $80–$201 suites.
Credit cards: American Express, Diners Club, MasterCard, Visa.
Restaurant and bar.
Spanish spoken.
Manager: Art Abbott.

---

**St. Anthony Hotel**
300 East Travis
San Antonio, Texas 78205
Telephone (512) 227-4392

"The St. Anthony is one of the last of the great old hotels of the
American Southwest. Recently refurbished, the narrow but ornate
marble lobby is a good place for an afternoon cocktail; the bar is
small but superb and the restaurants better than average. The larger
of the two restaurants serves Mexican specialties the day round, and
thus provides an interesting, if fiery, way to wake up at breakfast.
Accommodations are large and comfortable, although leaning toward the striped-wallpaper school of decor, and there are the usual
phones, color television, and air conditioning. The bathrooms are
huge and equipped with shower stalls as big as elevators. The staff
is mostly young and very competent, with a sprinkling of old Mexican retainers whom nothing, absolutely nothing, surprises. Room
service is above the usual horror, and there is parking on the premises."
                                                              —*L. J. Davis*

Open all year.
398 rooms, all with private bath.
Rates $65–$90 single, $85–$110 double.
Credit cards: American Express, Carte Blanche, Diners Club, Mas-
    terCard, Visa.
Manager: W. Andrews Kirmse.

All innkeepers appreciate reservations in advance; some require
them.

# Part Four

---

## Midwest

*Iowa*
*Minnesota*
*Missouri*
*Nebraska*

# Iowa

## Bentonsport

**Mason House Inn**
Front Street
Bentonsport, Iowa 52565
Telephone (319) 592-3133

The village of Bentonsport, an old steamboat stop on the Des Moines River, is now a National Historic District. Mason House Inn, built in 1846 as luxury accommodation for the better heeled among the passengers, is part of the history.

"This preserved 1840 village stands just as it did when the river was a bustling thoroughfare. The astonishing Mason House still has many rooms filled with original 1840–1870 furniture that helped make this one of the most luxurious hotels along the river. The hotel is owned by indomitable Burretta Redhead, who has fought long and hard to preserve this little chapter of the past. It is worth a visit any time of year." —*Jeanne Purdom*

"My wife and I found this to be everything we look for in a country inn. There is a great deal of history in the building and surrounding area, and Mr. and Mrs. Redhead were more than willing to tell us about it. Every room has been restored with great care. We were given a tour of the entire hotel and the outstanding General Store museum next door. We had a nice breakfast to send us off and the real, personal touch you hope for when visiting a country inn."

—*Mike McLain*

"Amish-style meals can be arranged if advance notice is given."

—*Mary Ovrom*

Open all year.
8 rooms sharing 3 baths, 1 cottage with bath.
Rates $30–$40, cottage $75 per day, including complete breakfast.
No credit cards.
No restaurant or bar.
Innkeepers: Herbert and Burretta Redhead.

## Homestead

### Die Heimat Motor Hotel
The Amana Colonies
Homestead, Iowa 52236
Telephone (319) 622-3937

*Heimat* means homeland in German, and Homestead, Iowa, was a small railhead village that became the seventh and last of the Amana Colonies, settlements founded by religious pilgrims of German, Swiss, and Alsatian background who came to Iowa in the mid-nineteenth century. The inn was built in 1858 as the communal kitchen, a role it played until 1932, when the religious Amana organization regrouped as a secular corporation. The building then became a boarding and apartment house. In 1964, four Amana men bought the house and made it the Heimat Motor Hotel. In 1975 the inn was taken over by Jim and Barbara Loyd, who now run it as a small hotel. From Die Heimat tourists can visit the restorations, shops, and restaurants of the Amana Colonies. There are also Amana museums and working industries to visit, including a hearth bakery, a woolen mill, a furniture and clock shop, and a smoke-house.

"Die Heimat is the only hotel in the Amana Colonies proper, and is easy to locate, though on a quiet street. This restored inn is furnished with lots of Amana furniture. The host-owners make all guests feel at home. We were served a very nice continental break-fast."

—*Captain and Mrs. James Blum*

Open all year.
18 rooms, all with private bath.
Rates $26–$30 double, $34–$40 twin, including continental break-
fast in busy months.
No credit cards.
No restaurant.
German spoken throughout Amana Colonies.
Innkeepers: Jim and Barbara Loyd.

## ————————————————————————— *Keosauqua*

**Hotel Manning**
Keosauqua, Iowa 52565
Telephone (319) 293-3232

Keosauqua, along with Bentonsport, Vernon, and Bonaparte, forms
part of a chain of interesting nineteenth-century Iowa river towns.
Connected by the Des Moines River, they are a historical center as
well as a base for year-round outdoor activities from canoeing to
cross-country skiing.

"Hotel Manning, on the bank of the Des Moines River, was constructed in 1839 as a general store to serve travelers in southeastern
Iowa. Later a second story was added, and the old red-brick building
became one of the first hotels for people traveling the river by
steamboat. Pillared and porticoed, it is known as a classic example
of Steamboat Gothic architecture. A rathskeller bar has been added,
with the original sandstone foundation and walls exposed. Guest
rooms are furnished in antiques, quilts, braided rugs, and chandeliers—but with all the modern conveniences. Motel accommodations are also available here for the less adventurous."

—*Mary Ovrom*

Open all year.
16 restored rooms, 6 motel units, all with private bath.
Rates $20–$33.50 single, $23–$36 double.
No credit cards.
Innkeepers: Darlene and Gerald Maas.

If you would like to amend, update, or disagree with any entry, write
*now.*

# _Minnesota_

## Baudette

**Rainy River Lodge**
Baudette, Minnesota 56623
Telephone (218) 634-2730

"When we go to the upper reaches of Minnesota, near the Canadian border, I choose the Rainy River Lodge, for two reasons: the hospitality of the place and the fishing. Not only are the food and cellar superb, but the rooms are also large and comfortable, commodious, and decorated, fortunately, with no interior decorators on the scene. Quality is the key word. As a fisherman, I think Rainy Lake is peerless." —_Dale E. Barlage_

Open May 15 to December 1.
5 cabins, all with private bath.
Rates $18–$45 per night, $108–$270 per week, including boat.
Credit cards: MasterCard, Visa.
Meals provided to guests on request.
Innkeepers: Linda and Ron Gores.

Turn to the back of this book for pages inviting _your_ comments.

# Grand Marais

**Cascade Lodge**
P.O. Box 693
Grand Marais, Minnesota 55604
Telephone (218) 387-1112

"While traveling on one of the continent's most scenic drives, from Duluth to Thunder Bay, Ontario, one must stop at Cascade Lodge, on the shores of Lake Superior. The activities here are varied, including hiking, stargazing, cross-country skiing, and searching for agates. And there is the mystique of the largest inland water in the world. The lodge, in existence for sixty years, does not allow liquor, and takes pride in its family atmosphere. The chef provides some of the best food between Duluth and Thunder Bay."

*—Dale E. Barlage*

Open all year.
13 rooms in lodge, 12 other units including 4 log cabins, all with
    private bath.
Rates $29–$49 single, $35–$55 double.
Credit cards: MasterCard, Visa.
Restaurant, but no bar.
Finnish and German spoken.
Triangle bus line connects to Duluth or Thunder Bay.
Innkeepers: Gene and Laurene Glader.

# Minneapolis

**Marquette**
710 Marquette Avenue, at IDS Center
Minneapolis, Minnesota 55402
Telephone (612) 332-2351

"Minneapolis is a world-class city, a state-of-the-art city. In the heartland of America, it has attracted worldwide attention with its two art museums, its Orchestra Hall, its Tyrone Guthrie Theater, and its vanguard zoo.

"In the urban heart of Minneapolis is a great little hotel, frequented by symphony buffs, scholars, artists, and connoisseurs of good food. The hotel's capacious rooms and public areas were designed by Philip Johnson, thus the guest has the chic and elegance of the Bauhaus style merged with the later internationalism of David Webb and his associates. All fit remarkably well. One can breakfast on the terrace overlooking America's answer to Milan's Galleria. Lunch and dinner are in the Marquis, a French restaurant. Room service is remarkably fleet.

"Father Marquette, a putative trencherman and man of grace, would have been delighted."    —*Dr. F. M. Hinkhouse*

Open all year.
282 rooms and suites, all with private bath.
Rates $85–$475.
Credit cards: American Express, Carte Blanche, Diners Club, MasterCard, Visa.
General Manager: Jephson Hilary.

_____*New Prague*

**Schumacher's New Prague Hotel**
212 West Main Street
New Prague, Minnesota 56071
Telephone (612) 758-2133

In a community with a largely Czech and German heritage, John and Nancy Schumacher have restored an 1898 hotel, decorating it with Bavarian folk art and giving the twelve rooms the names of the months of the year. Above the door of each room a glass medallion from Munich names the month.

"Only forty miles from Minneapolis, one feels one is in another part of the world. The clocks and woodcarvings are authentic Bavarian —it is like something out of a storybook.

"The food is excellent, all made with fresh eggs, pork, veal, vegetables, grains, and other ingredients from the surrounding area. The owner is also the chef. The specialties of the house are prepared with a German or Czech accent. Some of the entrées include sauerbraten, rabbit, wiener schnitzel, and many other wonderful veal dishes."    —*Dale E. Barlage*

Open all year, except 3 days at Christmas.
12 rooms, all with private bath.
Rates $60–$80.
No credit cards.
Innkeeper: John Schumacher.

Do you know a hotel in your state that we have overlooked? Write *now.*

_____*Red Wing*

**St. James Hotel**
406 Main Street
Red Wing, Minnesota 55066
Telephone (612) 388-2846

The St. James was built in 1875 when Red Wing had become the largest wheat market in the world and eleven local businessmen wanted to celebrate the city's success. The hotel was run by the Lillyblad family for seventy-two years. Legend is that Clara Lillyblad's food was so good that trains stopped in Red Wing just for a meal. The hotel was bought in 1975 by the Red Wing Shoe Company, which paid for an extensive restoration. The renewed hotel reopened in 1979.

"Red Wing is a Mississippi River town with a long history and many interesting old homes. Amtrak stops here, so if you like riding trains, this is a good location. By car, it is a beautiful ride along river bluffs. The guest rooms at the St. James have been faithfully refurnished and decorated in elegant Victorian style, with brass beds, lace-trimmed sheets, and beautiful furniture. There are fresh flowers in every room, and the beds are turned down nightly. The lobby, staircase, hallways, dining room, and library contain many exquisite antiques. I went to the St. James for a rest and enjoyed everything from the sound of the trains and river traffic to the silence of an old hotel content with its new lease on life."
—*Eileen R. McCormack*

Open all year.
60 rooms, all with private bath.
Rates $55–$80.
Credit cards: American Express, MasterCard, Visa.
3 restaurants and bar.
Red Wing reachable by train, Greyhound bus, and boat.
Innkeeper: Gene Foster.

_____*St. Paul*

**Bleick House**
270 Fort Road West
St. Paul, Minnesota 55102
Telephone (612) 227-2800

"We were in St. Paul on business when we decided to stay over a few days and just happened on this bed-and-breakfast inn in an older part of town where many homes have been restored. Bleick House is on the National Register. Within a block is another Victorian house serving food. The inn is within walking distance of all downtown St. Paul's museums, theaters, and stores."

—*Carol Kendrick*

Open all year.
22 rooms with shared baths.
Rates $25 single, $35 double, including breakfast.
Credit cards: MasterCard, Visa.
Innkeeper: Eleanor Saunders.

---

*Sauk Centre*

## Palmer House Hotel
500 Sinclair Lewis Avenue
Sauk Centre, Minnesota 56378
Telephone (612) 352-3431

Sauk Centre, at the southern end of Big Sauk Lake, was the childhood home of Sinclair Lewis, who was later to satirize small-town America in *Main Street.* Sauk Centre became his Gopher Prairie. Later in life he mellowed: among his lesser-known books is *Work of Art,* which praised the keeper of a small hotel. When Lewis died in Rome, his ashes were returned to his birthplace here. Both the Lewis home and a center devoted to the works of the United States' first Nobel Prize-winning novelist are open to the public in summer. The Palmer House, where Lewis worked in 1902 while still a boy and which barely escaped demolition ten years ago, has recently been listed in the National Register of Historic Places.

"There is much *here* to recall *Main Street.* In the hotel are two private party rooms, the Kennicott and the Minniemashie, both reminiscent of Lewis. The hotel was bought in 1974 by two men—a former Methodist minister and an ex-printer—tired of metropolitan living, who restored the old place to the way it was in the early 1900s, when Lewis worked here.

"I checked into the hotel quite by chance. I found no elegant decor, but the lack of luxury was immediately overcome by the hospitality that prevailed. Frequently, eight-course dinners are served, and all the meals are good."    —*Pauline Wilcox*

Open all year.
37 rooms, 4 with private bath.

Rates $15–$35.
No credit cards.
Restaurant; no bar, but beer and wine served.
German spoken.
Greyhound bus service.
Innkeepers: R. J. Schwartz and A. W. Tingley.

_____Stillwater

**Lowell Inn**
102 North Second Street
Stillwater, Minnesota 55082
Telephone (612) 439-1100

Lowell Inn has been owned or managed by the Palmer family since it opened in 1924. Arthur and Nelle, pianist and actress with a good deal of experience on the road, were the first Palmers to run the hotel, which they bought in 1945. The second and third generations are now in charge.

"The inn is a special place to stay for that special weekend. My husband and I have spent more than ten anniversary weekends—not to mention a honeymoon—there. Stillwater, the birthplace of Minnesota, is a beautiful little town north of St. Paul on the St. Croix River. It has a long history and is proud of it.

"The inn's lobby has generous overstuffed furniture arranged in comfortable groupings for conversation and cocktails while waiting for a table in one of the three dining rooms. The Washington Room is more formal, with white linen, silver, and china. The Garden Room has a stone floor, wrought-iron tables, and a natural spring waterfall. The third, the Matterhorn Room, is best of all: there is no menu, just fondue served with escargots, salad, dessert, and wine. All this is set in a room with exquisite Swiss wood carvings."

—*Margaret A. Levey*

Open all year.
17 rooms, 4 suites, all with private bath.
Rates $59–$109.
Credit cards: American Express, Diners Club, MasterCard, Visa.
Innkeepers: Arthur and Maureen Palmer.

All inkeepers appreciate reservations in advance; some require them.

_____ *Wabasha*

## Anderson House
333 West Main Street
Wabasha, Minnesota 55981
Telephone (612) 565-4003

"Established in 1856, the Anderson is Minnesota's oldest continuously operating hotel. It was recently designated a historic landmark. Except for a few years, the hotel has always been operated by the Anderson family, who came here from Pennsylvania. Over the years, they have wisely kept the hotel in its original state, with gorgeous furniture over a hundred years old. One room is called the Mayo, because doctors from the Mayo Clinic, forty miles away, frequently stayed there.

"Wabasha is an important city historically. It is seventy miles southeast of the Twin Cities, on the Mississippi River and on the direct route from Minneapolis to Chicago via Red Wing, Winona, LaCrosse, and Milwaukee. A bridge spans the Mississippi at Wabasha, so that one can drive on an equally fine highway to Chicago on the other side of the river. In the 1820s, Wabasha (or Wapasha, named for a Sioux chief) was an important fur-trading center. The unit of exchange—worth 5 cents—was the muskrat. The Grace Memorial Episcopal Church, given to the town by wealthy lumber people, is probably the most beautiful church in the world in a town this size. Designed by a New York architect, and possessing gorgeous Tiffany windows, the ninety-year-old church is in perfect condition. The *Delta Queen* and its new counterpart, the *Mississippi Queen,* make regular stops at Wabasha."     —*Dr. Harold C. Habein*

Open all year.
45 rooms, 20 with private bath.
Rates $16–$39. Package plans with meals available.
No credit cards.
Greyhound bus service.
Innkeeper: John Hall

Where are the good little hotels in Boston? Philadelphia? Omaha? Dallas? If you have found one, don't keep it a secret. Write *now.*

# Missouri

## Hermann

**Der Klingerbau Inn**
108 East Second Street
Hermann, Missouri 65041
Telephone (314) 486-2030

The celebration in 1983 of 300 years of German settlement in the United States brought attention not only to the widespread pioneering efforts of German immigrants but also to the strength of their traditions and the importance of their contribution to the development of the country. Everyone knows about German breweries, but fewer people associate these immigrants—as they do the French or Italians—with a fine wine culture. A visit to Hermann, on the banks of the Missouri River about seventy-five miles from St. Louis and forty-eight miles from Jefferson City, can fill that gap. This town of fewer than 3,000 people, a center of German settlement and viniculture, has been very busy restoring and preserving its history: there are two wineries, two historic districts, and over a hundred buildings on the National Register of Historic Places.

Hermann has several German-style festivals each year, and so there are bus tours. Visitors who want a quieter time may want to pick an in-between season. The people to consult about all of this are Bill and Betty Taylor, who have become something of a one-family chamber of commerce. They were known primarily as the owners of the Calico Cupboard, a restaurant, until a writer described their inn as having a *gasthaus* atmosphere and tourists began to arrive looking for rooms. There are still a few suites in the restaurant building, but the Taylors' main overnight business has moved to Der Klingerbau, a Victorian house built in 1878 for a German miller, William Klinger, by Otto Wilhelmi, an architect and interior designer who had just completed his studies in Karlsruhe. The Taylors, who bought the house in 1981, have been able to restore or salvage much of Wilhelmi's work. Rooms in the house are now named for local historical figures. In the last few years the Taylors have added several more nineteenth-century houses to their collection; these they prefer to rent as whole cottages.

"The Klingerbau Inn opened in 1982, and it is already a special place to visit. Betty and Bill Taylor spent many minutes talking about Hermann. The Calico Cupboard restaurant was reasonable, the food delicious. We plan to go back for a weekend to try the Sunday feast."                     —*Karl and Carol Brush*

Open all year.
6 rooms in inn, 2 suites at Calico Cupboard, 2 guesthouses—one sleeping 4–6 people, the other 6–8.
Rate $47.50 double, including breakfast. Rates including additional meals available in winter months.
Credit cards: American Express, MasterCard, Visa.
Amtrak stops in Hermann during October and May festivals. Inn will meet guests at municipal airport.
German spoken.
Innkeeper: Betty Taylor.

## St. Genevieve

**Hotel St. Genevieve**
Main and Merchant Streets
St. Genevieve, Missouri 63670
Telephone (314) 883-2737

Sixty miles south of St. Louis, this town is reputed to be the oldest French settlement west of the Mississippi. It has joined the growing number of small towns undergoing restoration; the antique shops are already flourishing. Although the Hotel St. Genevieve and its interior appear more Midwest Modern than period, the building is in the heart of the historic district.

"We were stranded in this historic town because of the weather. The hotel was such a friendly place, however, and we enjoyed the food and thought the Saturday night entertainment was great."
—*Carole Fuchs*

Open all year.
12 rooms, all with private bath.
Rates $22–$30.
Credit cards: MasterCard, Visa.
Restaurant and two lounges.
German and Spanish spoken.
Innkeeper: L. A. Becker.

# St. Louis

**Forest Park Hotel**
4910 West Pine Boulevard
St. Louis, Missouri 63108
Telephone (314) 361-3500

"The hotel is a good deal larger than it appears from the outside, yet smaller than one assumes from the spacious lobby. The decor is French Provincial in blue and gold, with many prints (Parisian scenes, Picassos and, alas, the inevitable Keanes). The rooms are large by American urban standards, and the rates are relatively low. There is free, secure parking across the street. The hotel restaurant competes with a good assortment of French, Italian, and seafood places in the area, which is away from downtown and in the section of the city that offers the best cultural and scenic advantages."
—*Shari and Berni Benstock*

"The hotel is close to the zoo, parks, and nice restaurants. They even have people operating the elevators, who say: 'watch your step.' "
—*Mark L. Goodman*

Open all year.
250 rooms and suites, all with private bath.
Rates $39 single, $45 double.
Credit cards: American Express, Carte Blanche, Diners Club, MasterCard, Visa.
Manager: George Richards.

# Nebraska

## Belgrade

**Bel-Horst Inn**
Belgrade, Nebraska 68623
Telephone (308) 357-1094

"Nestled in the Cedar River Valley of central Nebraska, Belgrade is a quaint and picturesque village with a unique attraction: the Bel-Horst Inn. Built in 1907 as the Andrews Hotel, it was used by railroaders and cattlemen. It became a victim of the 1930s drought and Depression, and sat vacant for forty years. A restoration project began in 1973, and now, when you push open the iron lobby door, you go back into turn-of-the-century decor. Each of the fourteen guest rooms is furnished with old wood and brass furniture. The bedspreads are exquisite piecework quilts. Lace curtains adorn the windows.

"In the lobby hang over 100 pictures of Belgrade residents and scenes. The dining room is set off by brass chandeliers and flowered glass. A private party room is furnished with antique kitchen and dining items. The cuisine is superb and reasonably priced. The inn recently escaped being auctioned because of a dispute between the

Horst brothers, who restored it. But that's been settled, and Richard
Horst is now the owner."                                    —*Joseph L. Neal*

"Here there was true small-town atmosphere—but no shower!"
                                                            —*Mark L. Goodman*

Open Friday and Saturday nights and Sunday until noon.
14 rooms, all with private bath.
Rate $20.
No credit cards.
Public bar and restaurant.
Innkeepers: Richard and Betty Horst.

## *Crawford*

**Fort Robinson**
Box 392
Crawford, Nebraska 69339
Telephone (308) 665-2660

"In the far northwest corner of Nebraska, just west of Crawford, lies
the old Fort Robinson Military Reservation. A very important cav-
alry post during the Indian wars, it was abandoned by the military
in 1948 and reverted to state control. In the 1960s the Nebraska
Game and Parks Commission took over the post and restored a
number of the remaining buildings; it has continued to expand the
facilities. One of the enlisted men's barracks has been converted to
a lodge with comfortable guest rooms, meeting rooms, and an excellent restaurant. The officers' adobe quarters have been made
into family units, and the large multifamily residences, built in the
early 1900s, are available for large groups. There is a great deal of
history and much scenic area around Fort Robinson."
                                                            —*Joseph L. Neal*

Open Memorial Day weekend to Labor Day weekend.
23 rooms, plus cabins and 5- to 9-bedroom officers' quarters.
Rates $12–$70 for larger buildings.
Credit cards: MasterCard, Visa.
Restaurant, no bar.
Superintendent: Vince Rotherham.

If you would like to amend, update, or disagree with any entry, write
*now*.

_____*Omaha*

## Granada Royale Hometel
7270 Cedar Street
Omaha, Nebraska 68124
Telephone (402) 397-5141

"Since the demise of the Blackstone, the Granada Royale has become the place to stay in Omaha. In the enclosed atrium, a virtual botanical garden of trees, shrubs, and foliage is the setting for evening cocktails—an experience further enhanced by the dulcet tones of a harpist. It is all grand, warm, and restful, as are the handsome suites that fortunately do remind one of Granada in Spain. The hand-carved, Spanish-style furniture and the tiled floors and dadoes are a delight to the optic nerve, just as breakfast by the Andalusian fountains is to the taste buds."

—*Dr. F. M. Hinkhouse*

Open all year.
191 suites, all with private bath and kitchenette.
Rate $79 double, including full breakfast and complimentary afternoon cocktails.
Credit cards: American Express, Carte Blanche, Diners Club, MasterCard, Visa.
Free limousine service to Eppley Airfield.
General Manager: Arlene Vander-Vegt.

Details of special features offered by an inn or hotel vary according to information supplied by the hotels themselves. The absence here of a recreational amenity, a bar, or a restaurant doesn't necessarily mean one of these doesn't exist. Ask the innkeeper when booking your room.

# Part Five

## South
### Louisiana

# _Louisiana_

## New Orleans

### French Quarter Maisonettes
1130 Chartres Street
New Orleans, Louisiana 70116
Telephone (504) 524-9918

"Innkeeper Mrs. Junius Underwood and her two cats make a stay here an absolute delight. Inside the clean apartment and snug courtyard it was hard to imagine we were in the heart of the French Quarter. Mrs. Underwood gives each guest an excellent folder that includes suggestions for restaurants, things to do, and tours."
—_Jack and Sue Lane_

Open all year, except July.
7 rooms and suites, all with private bath.
Rates $38–$44.
No credit cards.
Innkeeper: Mrs. Junius Underwood.

Rates quoted were the latest available. But they may not reflect unexpected increases or local and state taxes. Be sure to verify when you book.

## Lafitte Guest House
1003 Bourbon Street
New Orleans, Louisiana 70116
Telephone (504) 581-2678

Acquired by its present owners in 1980, the house had been taking in guests for many years with what the manager, Steve Guyton, calls "varying degrees of success and popularity." Mr. Guyton has been at work for several years on restoration and redecoration of the house, which was built in the French style in 1849 for Paul Joseph Geleises—a wealthy man, judging by the cost of construction. The house, in the city's historic district, the Vieux Carré, was built on a site that had been occupied by one building or another since 1795.

"Nestled in the heart of this beautiful and historic city amid some of the most popular nightspots in America, the Lafitte Guest House nonetheless seems miles from the clamor and buzz of the French Quarter. This old building offers the finest lodgings we have found in the city. Decor is exquisite: a fine eclectic mixture of lovely Victorian antiques and contemporary textures and tones.

"Just outside the door is Bourbon Street and all you have ever heard about it. Within easy walking distance are some of the world's greatest restaurants, the city's business district, and the Mississippi River. Canal Street separates the old from the older. A streetcar ride up St. Charles Avenue passes some of the most splendid Greek Revival palaces of the South."     —*Catherine and Bill Bailey Carter*

Open all year.
14 rooms, all with private bath.
Rates $58–$85 single, $68–$95 double, including continental breakfast.
Credit cards: American Express, MasterCard, Visa.
No restaurant or bar.
Airport limousine service available.
Manager: Steve Guyton.

## Lamothe House
621 Esplanade Avenue
New Orleans, Louisiana 70116
Telephone (504) 947-1161

This house was built in about 1800 for Jean Lamothe, a wealthy French sugar planter from Santo Domingo, who was seeking a safe place for his family because of disturbances on the island. It became a guesthouse in the 1950s.

"Walking through the entrance hall, you are confronted by a patio with three stories of balconies, a fishpond, and lots of plants. Ascending the curved stair, you are welcomed by the innkeeper or a member of the staff. A visit to the French Quarter is much enhanced by a visit to this inn."   *—James K. Mellow*

"The continental breakfast in the dining room was a daily high point, since we met and chatted with some very interesting guests. Offstreet parking here is another boon."   *—Marion Smith*

Open all year.
16 rooms and suites, all with private bath.
Rates $75–$100, including continental breakfast.
Credit cards: American Express, MasterCard, Visa.
Airport limousine service; local buses for touring city.
Innkeepers: Frieda and Ralph Lutin.

---

**Maison de Ville**
727 Toulouse Street
New Orleans, Louisiana 70130
Telephone (504) 561-5858

"It is easy to overlook the sign at 727 Toulouse Street. Maybe that is as it should be. Once inside, it is even easier to overlook the fact that you are in a hotel. The building was a home from the early nineteenth century until the late 1930s. The conversion to a well-maintained hotel offering modern comforts had been achieved without changes in appearance. Furnishings are authentic to private homes in early nineteenth-century New Orleans. The courtyard, with its fountain in the center and its slave quarters that have been converted to guest rooms, is a delightful spot for your breakfast, afternoon tea, or evening port.

"The sightseer could not find a more convenient location. A half-block to the left and you are in the fine shopping area of Royal Street. A half-block to the right and you are in the heart of Bourbon Street night life, which really is in full swing around the clock. Some of the finest restaurants are within three blocks. The staff can make reservations for dining: they seem to be on a first-name basis with the restaurants, and get you a good table."

—*John B. Parramore, Jr.*

"The variety of the restaurants is exceptional. Across the street from the Maison de Ville is a pub called Molly's, where we enjoyed barbecue and beans. More elegant is the food at Le Ruth's in Gretna, across the river—but reservations are needed long in advance. Another favorite is the Caribbean Room at the Hotel Ponchartrain. Try Crozier's, too. And the K-Paul is fun."

—*Art and Susan Bachrach*

"We had a gorgeous suite in the Audubon cottage—a heavenly oasis."                                             —*Camille J. Cook*

Open all year.
21 rooms, all with private bath.
Rates $80–$95 single, $90–$105 double, including continental
    breakfast.
No credit cards.
Manager: William W. Prentiss.

---

## Olivier House
828 Toulouse Street
New Orleans, Louisiana 70112
Telephone (504) 525-8456

"The Olivier House is in the French Quarter, the old Franco-Spanish city of the Creoles. Most tourist attractions—as well as historic sites such as St. Louis Cathedral, Jackson Square, the Cabildo Museum, the Jazz Museum, and the Pontalba Apartments—are within a four-block range. The hotel was built in 1836 as a town house for the widow of Nicolas Olivier, a wealthy plantation owner. The major part of the hotel consists of the old Olivier home with the slave quarters in the back."                    —*John and Jeannette Holt*

"My husband and I spent a marvelous four days here. The room we had was furnished with antiques, and the staff left it spick-and-span every morning. There were rolls and coffee for breakfast and a crème de menthe candy on each pillow at night. The atmosphere was one of a home. The resident cat even had kittens during our stay. Our visit spoiled us as to what kind of hotels we will stay in from now on."                                    —*Nancy L. Kuethe*

"We selected the Olivier House from this book, made reservations two months in advance, and were confirmed for a brass bed, balcony, and so on. The airport limo dropped us there on a Friday night, and what were we shown? A back room with a two-by-four window and an unmade bed. Our first evening in New Orleans was spent walking the streets looking for another place to stay. We suggest removing this one."   —*Jack and Sue Lane*

Open all year.
40 rooms, including 7 suites, all with private bath.
Rates $50–$95.
Credit cards: American Express, MasterCard, Visa.
No restaurant or bar.
Spanish spoken.
Innkeepers: Jim and Kathy Danner.

# St. Francisville

## The Cottage Plantation
Route 5 (P.O. Box 425)
St. Francisville, Louisiana 70775
Telephone (504) 635-3674

The owners of this estate, built over a period from 1795 to 1850, believe that it is one of only a few antebellum plantations in the South to have remained intact in the post–Civil War period.

"The entire area up the Mississippi from Baton Rouge is full of history, and the Cottage Plantation is part of it. The annual Audubon Pilgrimage in St. Francisville includes this home, where Andrew Jackson and his men stayed en route to Natchez from the Battle of New Orleans. Hanging moss from giant live oak branches envelops the front gallery. At night the silence can be heard."
—*Charles L. Hoke*

"This is one of only a few plantation homes to take guests. Much intelligence has been used to retain the plantation's air of having been lived in, rather than done over and put back together. Every morning at 8, demitasses are brought to your room. Breakfast at 8:30 is taken in the beautiful dining room, overlooking the shaded veranda and lawn. No other food is available here, but lunch can be managed at one or two little places on the outskirts of St. Francisville. Dinner (and lunch, too) can be found at a nice old thirties sort of roadhouse called South of the Border—the Mississippi border, it turns out—or at Asphodel, about twenty miles back through town.

  "The area has many rehabilitated plantation houses open to the

public. One of the nicest is Oakley House, now a museum and state park. It is a large house where John J. Audubon lived and tutored for some years, while doing many of his famous bird paintings."
— *Will and Tedda Sternberg; also recommended by Marion Smith and Genevieve and Morrell Feltus Trimble*

Open all year, except Christmas Day.
5 rooms, all with private bath.
Rates $40 single, $60 twin or double, including morning coffee and full plantation breakfast.
No restaurant or bar.
Innkeeper: Mrs. Robert H. Weller.

---

**Propinquity**
523 Royal Street (P.O. Box 814)
St. Francisville, Louisiana 70775
Telephone (504) 635-6855

"St. Francisville, quiet and sleepy, is one of the most charming old towns of the South. The majority of the old homes are lived in, and if the owners wish to show them to the public, they place an 'Open' sign on the building. That's how we found Propinquity. The house is of Spanish design, built high, with two porches across the east exposure to catch the breeze. This was innkeeper Gladys Seif's childhood home."                    — *Mr. and Mrs. Ralph E. Heasley*

"We occupied the entire upstairs suite and were delighted with both our hosts and our accommodation. The Seifs are very active octogenarians who, when we visited, were preparing a crawfish party for 300 guests. We went on from here to Natchez, then on our return stayed again with the Seifs. Mrs. Seif gave us a tour of her home, and Mr. Seif took our picture, a practice by which they remember all their guests."                        — *Marion Smith*

Open all year, except Christmas and New Year's Day.
1 two-bedroom suite, with large bath.
Rate $50 double for each bedroom, including continental breakfast.
No credit cards.
No restaurant or bar.
Innkeepers: Charles and Gladys Seif.

Turn to the back of this book for pages inviting *your* comments.

# Part Six

## Canada

*British Columbia*
*Ontario*

*Qualicum College Inn,*
*Qualicum Beach*

# British Columbia

## Harrison Hot Springs

**The Harrison Hotel**
Harrison Hot Springs, British Columbia VOM 1KO
Telephone (604) 796-2244

"The old and the new are in delightful juxtaposition at Harrison Hot Springs in the Coast Ranges of the Canadian Rockies. There, the old timbered and the new stone structures are married in a setting beside a lake of near cobalt. The hotel, the quasi-village, and the unifying beach are surrounded by mountains. From your terrace you can breakfast or take cocktails and look out on a vast expanse of glistening water toward the distant Canadian Rockies.

"If time is a major problem, you can fly your plane to the airstrip behind the hotel, or you can land a seaplane directly in front. The hotel's staff are accustomed to fetching international guests fore or aft, and will give an appropriate welcome.

"Rooms in the old wing are capacious and high-ceilinged; the new wing tends to be motelesque but quiet and comfortable. In either facility room service is swift, smart, and gracious."

—*Dr. F. M. Hinkhouse*

Open all year.
278 rooms, all with private bath.

Rates $60–$80.
Credit cards: American Express, Carte Blanche, Chargex, Master-
Card, Visa.
Bus service from Vancouver.
Manager: David Campbell.

## Kelowna

### Lake Okanagan Resort
Mill 11 Westside Road (Box 1321, Station A)
Kelowna, British Columbia V1Y 7V8

"This tennis resort combines beautiful scenery, great facilities for
tennis, and boating in the most rustic of settings. Accommodations
in either town houses or flats with kitchens and washer-dryers allow
family vacations in a luxury area."                      —*Gwen Hudson*

Open March 15 to October 31.
200 rooms, all with private bath.
Rates $40–$125. Packages with meals available.
Credit cards: American Express, MasterCard, Visa.
General Manager: Leslie Szabo.

## Qualicum Beach

### Qualicum College Inn
P.O. Box 99
Qualicum Beach, British Columbia V0R 2T0
Telephone (604) 752-9262

"Qualicum College Inn—once a private boys' school—is on the east
coast of Vancouver Island, nestled among countryside thickets just
beyond a rolling green golf course overlooking the strait. You enter
the inn through castle doors. The reception area has handcrafted
medieval-style decor. Each of the bedrooms is identified by the
name of a British royal-family member. Just off the lobby is a library–sitting room. Pictures of classroom activities, of tournaments
played and trophies won, are arranged on the walls, along with
other mementos of the good old days when Qualicum was an exclusive boarding school. You frequently come across entrances marked
Headmaster, Gymnasium, or Laboratory. Down a winding red-car-
peted stairway is a candlelit dining room, where an internationally
accredited chef, the pride of the inn, treats his guests to his favorite
selections of dishes—among them a seven-course medieval meal.

What a treat it is to spend a long summer evening dining on the seaside patio. A leisurely whirlpool or sauna, a refreshing dip in the heated pool, a bit of classy disco music on weekends, and a nice tall nightcap in the lounge give a perfect end to any day."

—*Mary-Ann Tinney*

Open all year.
50 rooms, 49 with private bath.
Rates $36–$52 (Canadian dollars).
Credit cards: MasterCard, Visa.
Guests can be met at bus, plane, or train.
Innkeeper: Kerry Keilty.

## *Vancouver*

### The Four Seasons Vancouver
791 West Georgia
Vancouver, British Columbia V6C 2T4
Telephone (604) 689-9333

"The Four Seasons Vancouver is a hotel of ideal proportions for the guest, be he from the Yukon (in town shopping at the Hudson's Bay Company next door) or from the United States. The rooms are decidedly comfortable; their views of the maritime and urban life of this aquatic city—perhaps the San Francisco of Canada—are peerless and seemingly endless. This is not a cliché-ridden hotel. Instead one finds quiet, luxury, and abundant good taste. In the dining room a masterfully varied and enticing cuisine is prepared by savants of the culinary arts. After a swim in the covered-cum-uncovered pool high above the teeming streets one can enjoy an al fresco luncheon on the adjacent terrace to the tinkling waters of a Japanese garden. A sauna and workout facilities are available for those who want to steel themselves for yet another major meal in the Pavilion, by the Garden Court. The latter, sun-filled during Vancouver's better days, is a late twentieth-century adaptation of a Victorian winter garden; there one can take tea, an aperitif, or a paper-thin cucumber or watercress sandwich."   —*Dr. F. M. Hinkhouse*

Open all year.
434 rooms, all with private bath.
Rates $115–$130 single, $135–$150 double (Canadian dollars).
Credit cards: American Express, Diners Club, MasterCard, Visa.
General Manager: Peter G. Martin.

Rates for Canadian entries are quoted in Canadian dollars

_____ *Victoria*

## Olde England Inn
429 Lampson Street
Victoria, British Columbia V9A 5Y9
Telephone (604) 388-4353

"Take seven and a quarter square miles of England, place it in western Canada and you have the city of Victoria, capital of British Columbia. Carve out five acres of Elizabethan England and you have the Olde England Inn, as charming a hotel as one could find anywhere in the Mother Country. The beamed and paneled baronial entrance hall is graced not only by suits of armor and ancient swords but also by a refectory table upon which Charlotte and Emily Brontë supped.

"The inn is owned by Rosina Lane who, with her late husband, RAF Squadron Leader Sam Lane, migrated from Yorkshire in 1946, bringing with them seven tons of antiques. Other pieces of priceless silverware, china, and objets d'art were added later. In addition to the Kings' Rooms, there are other guest accommodations furnished in seventeenth-century antiques.

"Two attractive dining rooms specialize in typical English fare: roast beef with Yorkshire pudding, steak and kidney 'pye,' crumpets, scones, and sherry trifle, as well as local salmon and Alberta steaks.

"An integral part of the scene is the Olde English Village, a collection of buildings that includes an Olde Curiosity Shoppe, as immortalized by Charles Dickens, where treasures, old and new, are sold. The highlights of the village are the replicas of William Shakespeare's birthplace and Anne Hathaway's cottage."

*—Jayne and Arthur H. Elwood*

Open all year.
50 rooms, all with private bath.
Rates $45–$110, depending on antiques in room.
Credit cards: American Express, Diners Club, MasterCard, Visa.
Innkeeper: Cyril Lane.

All inkeepers appreciate reservations in advance; some require them.

# Ontario

## Algonquin Park

**Arowhon Pines**
Huntsville P.O.
Ontario POA 1KO
Telephone (705) 633-5661

"The Pines, as friends call it, rarely advertises in any medium more international than *The Toronto Globe and Mail,* but Europeans and North Americans who find it learn about it through word of mouth. Innkeepers Eugene and Helen Kates adhere to one of Eugene's gruff-voiced tenets: 'Look,' he rumbles, 'we're in the business of selling three things: a bedroom, a dining room, and a setting. The setting is superb'—he's right: the Pines adjoins a lake near the southern corner of a 3,000-square-mile provincial park that is a favorite of Canadian naturalists, canoe-trippers, and landscape painters—"but that's beyond our control, so we have to do our best with the other two.'

"The broad, hexagonal dining room, jutting over the lake, was built in the late 1930s by two brothers, Paul and Jack Lucasavitch. Of necessity they used only hand tools, plus a team of horses to winch into place the enormous central cast-iron chimney. Still solid as Canadian Shield granite, their construction has been applauded in several books on fine log buildings. As for its wares, the Pines' baker produces fresh breads and cakes daily, and each summer the Kateses have managed to steal yet another bright young chef from some major Toronto restaurant: their reputation for food has gone consistently up. (N.B. The sale of alcohol is forbidden in Ontario's parks. If you want wine with your meals—and they deserve it—you must bring your own. The hotel provides stemware, mixers, and corkscrews.) Fifty bedrooms are clustered in small buildings scattered through the densely wooded grounds. Each cabin has a common lounge area with a fireplace, comfortable chairs and sofas, a small refrigerator, and an eclectic collection of books. Helen Kates is a compulsive antiques hunter, so many of those stripped-pine pieces are authentic 'old Canada.'

"Canoeing is our recreation of choice. There's an easy but fun white-water creek leading to the Pines' lake from one to the north. There are wolf howls at night, loon calls at dawn. We've seen dozens of bird species, bears on almost every trip, and twice a moose. The canoes are free. So are the tennis and shuffleboard courts, rowboats, small sailboats, swim docks, picnic lunches, and well-marked trails through the bush. There is a small charge for outboard motor–equipped fishing boats and for baby-sitting. No tipping: *servis compris.*"   —*Mechtild Hoppenrath and Charles Oberdorf*

Open mid-May to mid-October.
49 rooms, all with private bath.
Rates $82.50–$165 single, $66–$126.50 double per person, AP. (Prices quoted are Canadian dollars.)
No credit cards.
Winter address for correspondence: 147 Davenport Road, Toronto M5R 1J1. Winter telephone: (416) 923-7176.
Innkeepers: Eugene and Helen Kates.

--------------------------------------------------*Alton*

**The Millcroft Inn**
John Street (Box 89)
Alton, Ontario L0N 1A0
Telephone (416) 791-4422

"Toronto's most elegant country retreat was created several years ago out of an old knitting mill, $3 million, and a lot of imagination. To ensure quality, the hotel is managed—though not owned—by the people from the Windsor Arms Hotel, in Toronto. Rooms in 'the Mill,' all twenty-two of them, are furnished with Canadian antiques. The twenty crofts on the hill are a longer walk from the heart of things—from the tennis courts, the outdoor pool, the bar, and the dining areas. Management by the Windsor Arms Hotel guarantees above all fine food imaginatively prepared: homemade sherbets and ices, salads of such uncommon ingredients as celery root, perfect drinks, vegetables grown in the inn's own garden and often picked moments before serving. Meals are not cheap. But many Toronto food fanatics drive two hours for the pleasure of eating there, without even spending the night." —*Mechtild Hoppenrath and Charles Oberdorf*

Open all year.
42 rooms, all with private bath.
Rates $90–$100.
Credit cards: American Express, Diners Club, MasterCard, Visa.
French, German, and Spanish spoken.
Gray Coach buses to Orangeville, taxis to Alton.
Innkeeper: Peter Chlup.

*Elora*

**The Elora Mill**
77 Mill Street West (Box 218)
Elora, Ontario N0B 1S0
Telephone (519) 846-5356

"Until 1973 this hotel was known as Drimmies Mill, a gristmill powered by the thundering waterfall that now crashes past the best tables in the cocktail lounge. Two families bought and refitted the old mill, transforming it into the crown jewel of this town of 2,500, which had already attracted a fair number of Sunday drivers with its artists' and craftsmen's workshops, its natural setting (hard by a deep limestone gorge full of caves, waterfalls, and rapids), and the beautiful surrounding countryside, largely farmed by buggy-driving Mennonites. We prefer the food at the less expensive, Basque-style Café Flore, just down the street, to dinners at the Mill. Or we go on a Saturday and assemble lunch from the Mennonite farmers' markets in nearby Kitchener and Elmira. In August, the town of Fergus, just down the road, stages one of Canada's more important festivals of 'highland games,' complete with bagpipes and flying cabers. In winter the Elora Gorge Conservation Area becomes one of the province's best cross-country skiing areas, the better for knowing that the Mill will have a nice hot buttered rum on hand at the end of the run."    —*Mechtild Hoppenrath and Charles Oberdorf*

Open all year.
20 rooms all with private bath.
Rates $60–$80.
Credit cards: American Express, MasterCard, Visa.
Train and bus service to Guelph, 11 miles away.
Innkeeper: Crozier Taylor.

# Hamilton

**Royal Connaught Hotel**
112 King Street East
Hamilton, Ontario L8N 1A8
Telephone (416) 527-5071

"The hotel is centrally located on King Street. It has a nice atmosphere; spacious, modern, well-appointed rooms. The staff is attentive, particularly in the dining room and at the reception desk."
—*H. C. Beddington*

Open all year.
215 rooms, all with private bath.
Rates from $60 single, $66 double.
Credit cards: American Express, Carte Blanche, Diners Club, En Route, MasterCard, Visa.
Manager: Barry Massey.

# Niagara-on-the Lake

**The Pillar and Post Inn**
48 John Street (Box 1011)
Niagara-on-the-Lake, Ontario L0S 1J0
Telephone (416) 468-2123

"This inn is less historically authentic than others in the town. It's a fairly recent recycling of an old industrial building, with all the modern conveniences like sauna and outdoor pool and mostly 'reproduction antiques' in the rooms. But it does have pretty quilts and fireplaces in some bedrooms."    —*Mechtild Hoppenrath and Charles Oberdorf*

"A nice pool, pretty flowers, and an excellent breakfast buffet. A special treat for us was that it was across from the yacht boatyards."
—*Dr. and Mrs. Michael Durishin*

Open all year.
91 rooms, all with private bath.
Rates $80–$90.
Credit cards: American Express, MasterCard, Visa.
Innkeeper: Neil O. Foster.

---

## Prince of Wales Hotel
6 Picton Street (Box 46)
Niagara-on-the-Lake, Ontario L0S 1J0
Telephone (416) 468-3246

"Dining adequately is no problem anywhere in Niagara-on-the-Lake, but dining splendidly is impossible. To the extent that it still reflects some excellent past management—by the Toronto consultants Nicholas Pearce and David Barrette—the Prince of Wales remains the best place to eat. A restored and enlarged hotel of Victorian vintage, the closest one to the Shaw theater, it is also a reasonable place to sleep. In any town this size, it would be a treasure."    —*Mechtild Hoppenrath and Charles Oberdorf*

"I agree with your evaluation of dinner."    —*Mary Jane Durishin*

Open all year.
87 rooms, 7 suites all with private bath.
Rates $65–$70 single, $70–$80 double, $85–$135 suites.
Credit cards: American Express, MasterCard, Visa.
French and German spoken.
Innkeepers: Henry and John Wiens.

---

*Toronto*

## King Edward Hotel
37 King Street East
Toronto, Ontario M5C 1E9
Telephone (416) 863-9700

"If you are headed for the center of the business district, there is no better hotel than the King Edward. The solid grandeur has been strikingly updated in a counterpoint that plays the freshness and openness of modern taste against the muted background of elaborate ornamentation. Decor is a triumph. Service is a close second."

*—George Herzog*

Open all year.
290 rooms, 30 suites, all with private bath.
Rates $98–$155 single, $118–$175 double (Canadian currency).
Credit cards: American Express, Diners Club, En Route, Master-Card, Visa.
Eight languages spoken by the concierge.
General Manager: Mr. I. Fahmy.

---

## Park Plaza Hotel
4 Avenue Road
Toronto, Ontario M5R 2E8
Telephone (416) 924-5471

"The Park Plaza is of the same chain as the Inn on the Park in London. No rooms, only suites. The hotel has a delightful atmosphere, is well appointed and well located."   *—H. C. Beddington*

Open all year.
340 rooms, all with private bath.
Rates $80–$90 single, $95–$105 double.
Credit cards: Air Canada, American Express, Diners Club, Master-Card, Visa.
French and many other languages spoken.
Manager: Konrad Steger.

---

## The Windsor Arms Hotel
22 St. Thomas Street
Toronto, Ontario M5S 2B9
Telephone (416) 979-2341

"Booking into the Windsor Arms means sharing the taste of Pierre Trudeau and Katharine Hepburn. A little gem of a Tudor-style palace, it nestles quietly off the trafficked streets, yet is just a block from the most elegant shopping of Yorkville and the Royal Ontario Museum. Rooms have been restored and redecorated in warm colors. Furnishings range from late Regency to a 1920s variety of

English Renaissance, with an occasional brass bed. My room was graced with a sitting alcove that had a charming settee and a beautiful wall of cupboards with leaded-glass fronts. The cupboards, alas, were bare—but bare was the last thing that could be said of the garden that provisions the hotel's several fine restaurants, among the best in Toronto. If you want a small taste of British-Canadian tradition, treat yourself to kippers at breakfast."    —*George Herzog*

Open all year.
81 rooms, 25 with shower, 56 with bath and shower.
Rates $65–$275.
Credit cards: American Express, Carte Blanche, Diners Club, MasterCard, Visa.
French spoken.
Near train and bus stations.
Innkeeper: Norbert Ackerman.

Would you be so kind as to share discoveries you may have of charming, well-run places to stay in Europe? Please write to *Europe's Wonderful Little Hotels and Inns,* c/o Congdon & Weed, 298 Fifth Avenue, New York, New York 10001. (By the way, a new and greatly expanded edition of this splendid guide is now available at your bookseller's.)

_____ *Maps*

OREGON

IDAHO

Eureka
5
Ferndale
Garberville
Piercy
Mendocino
Anchor Bay
Gualala
Cloverdale
Calistoga
Saint Helena
Nevada City
NEVADA
Great Salt Lake
80
Salt Lake City
Midway
Yountville
Sacramento
Gold Hill (Virginia City)
UTAH
Point
Reyes
Station
Sutter Creek
Murphys
Napa
Mokelumne Hill
70
Boyes
Hot
Sausalito
Columbia
Springs
San Francisco
Yosemite
15
Aptos
99
Pacific
Grove
Monterey
Carmel
101
Big
Sur
Reedley
CALIFORNIA
San Luis
Obispo
5
Los Alamos
Santa Barbara
Grand Canyon
Beverly Hills
40
ARIZONA
PACIFIC
OCEAN
Seal Beach
Laguna Beach
10
Paradise Valley
17
Rancho Santa Fe
Scottsdale
La Jolla
San Diego
Litchfield Park
Coronado
8
MEXICO
Tucson
10
Cochise

0   50  100        200 Miles
0      100       200 Kilometers

N
W        E
S

PACIFIC
OCEAN

Honolulu

HAWAII

Kailua-Kona
Hawaii Volcanoes
National Park

0        50       100 Miles
0      50      100 Kilometers

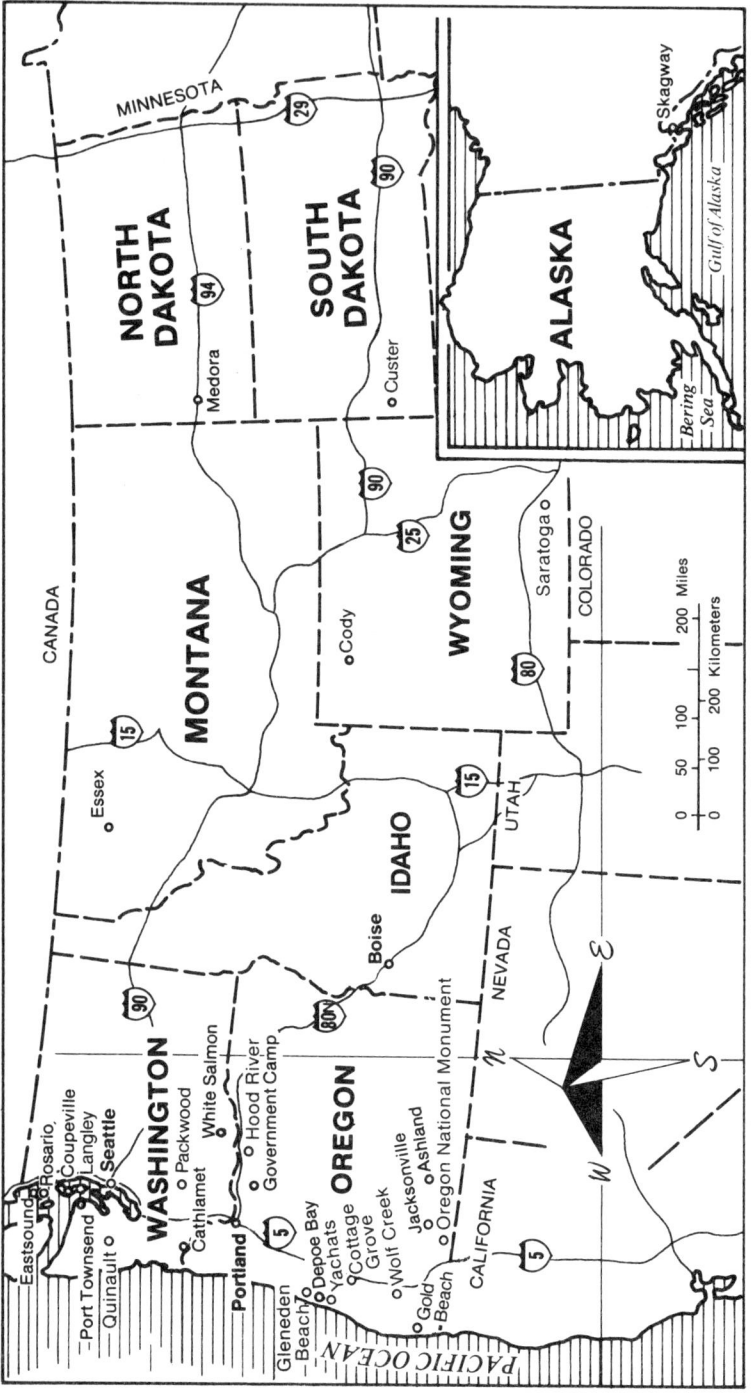

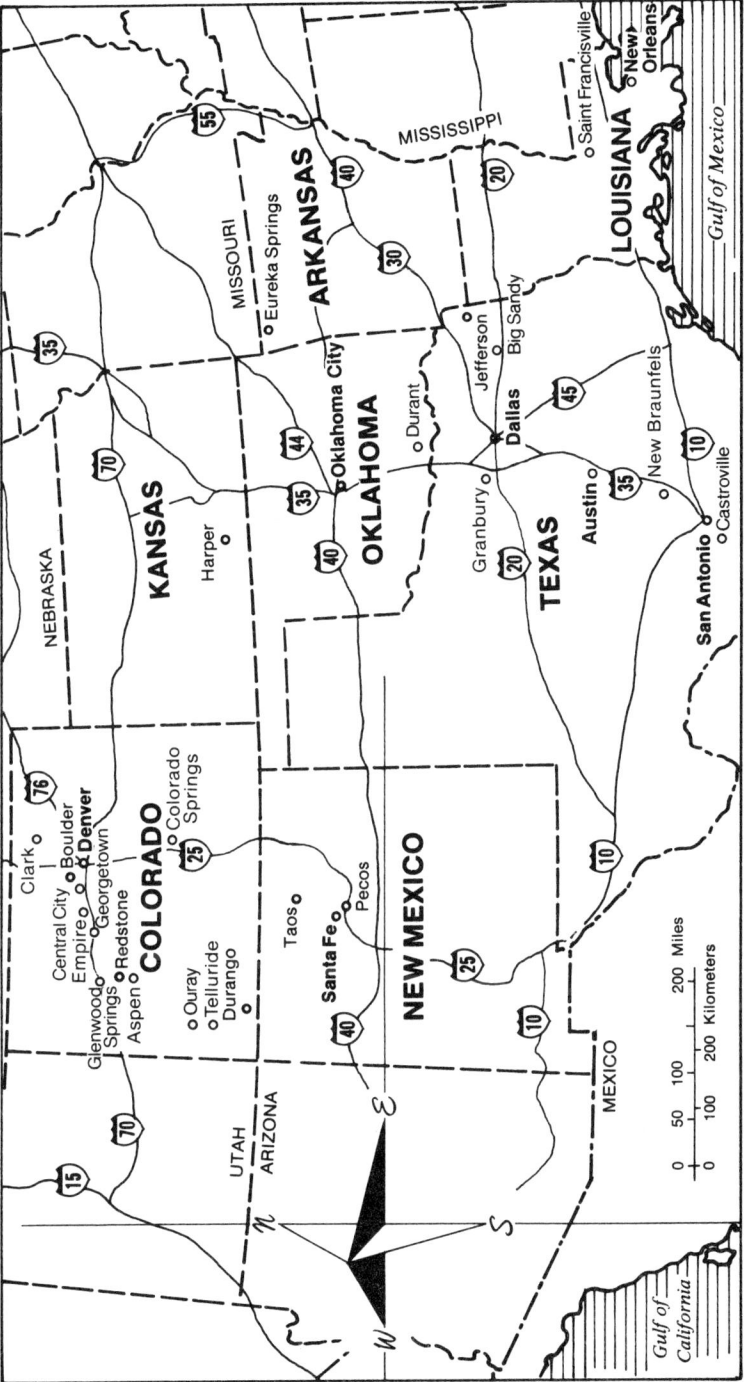

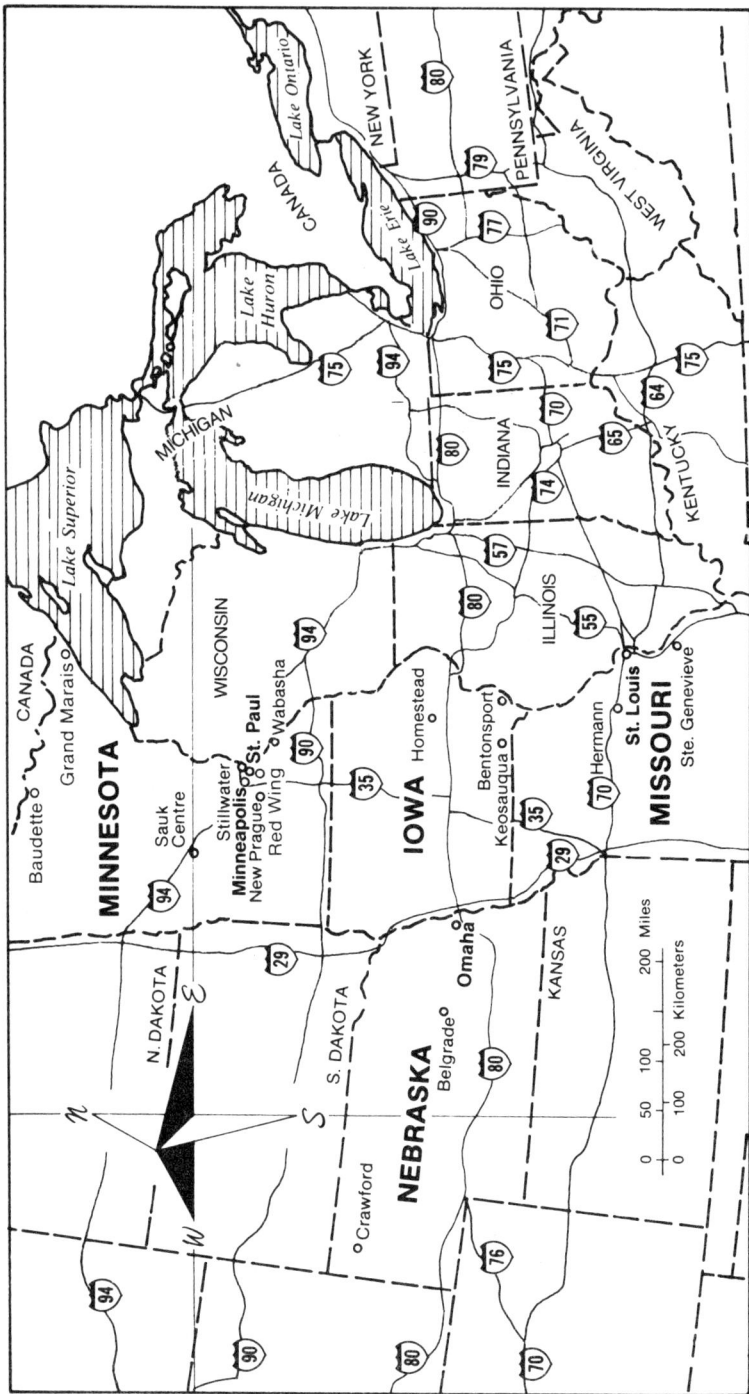

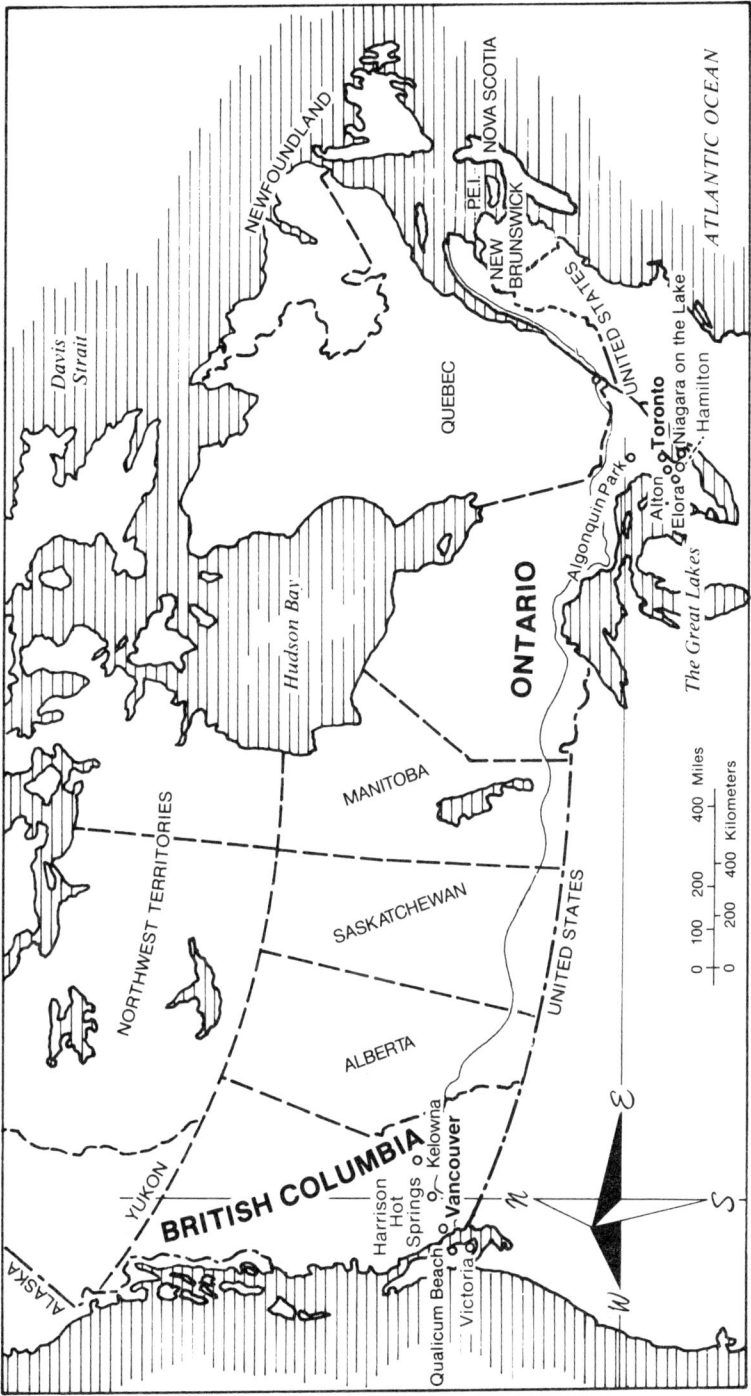

# *Hotel*
## *Reports*

The pages that follow are for you to use to amend, criticize, or update entries in this book, or to suggest new entries for our next edition. When you nominate a hotel or inn, please tell other travelers about the region or neighborhood as well as the hotel itself; this is particularly helpful when you write about areas of the country not familiar to many people. There is no need to include a lot of factual information (prices, number of rooms, etc.) with your entry; this is supplied by the hotels and inns. What you will give us is the spirit and character of the places you find. There is no need to confine your comments to a single page. It is important that you send your comments soon, so that this guide can be kept as up-to-date as possible. And thank you for sharing your finds with other people like yourself.

**To:**

**The Editor**
*America's Wonderful Little Hotels and Inns*
**Congdon & Weed, Inc.**
**298 Fifth Avenue**
**New York, N.Y. 10001**

Name of Hotel _____

Address _____

_____

Date of most recent visit _____ Duration of visit _____

☐ New recommendation      ☐ Comment on existing entry

In addition to a description of the inn and its setting, your room, the food, and some of the nearby sights, we'd like to hear about your comfort (or discomfort) during your stay—cleanliness, service, lighting, plumbing, parking, quiet, etc.—and the quality of the welcome and hospitality you received.

Report:

Signed _____

Name and address (please print) _____

_____

_____

**To:**
**The Editor**
*America's Wonderful Little Hotels and Inns*
**Congdon & Weed, Inc.**
**298 Fifth Avenue**
**New York, N.Y. 10001**

Name of Hotel _____
Address _____

Date of most recent visit _____ Duration of visit _____
☐ New recommendation ☐ Comment on existing entry

In addition to a description of the inn and its setting, your room, the food, and some of the nearby sights, we'd like to hear about your comfort (or discomfort) during your stay—cleanliness, service, lighting, plumbing, parking, quiet, etc.—and the quality of the welcome and hospitality you received.

Report:

Signed _____

Name and address (please print) _____

_____

_____

**To:**
  **The Editor**
  *America's Wonderful Little Hotels and Inns*
  **Congdon & Weed, Inc.**
  **298 Fifth Avenue**
  **New York, N.Y. 10001**

Name of Hotel _____
Address _____
_____
Date of most recent visit _____ Duration of visit _____
☐ New recommendation          ☐ Comment on existing entry

In addition to a description of the inn and its setting, your room, the food, and some of the nearby sights, we'd like to hear about your comfort (or discomfort) during your stay—cleanliness, service, lighting, plumbing, parking, quiet, etc.—and the quality of the welcome and hospitality you received.

Report:

Signed _____

Name and address (please print) _____
_____
_____

# Index by State

ALASKA

Skagway Inn, Skagway 73

ARIZONA

Arizona Biltmore, Phoenix 6
Arizona Inn, Tucson 8
The Cochise Hotel, Cochise 3
El Tovar Hotel, Grand Canyon
    4
Hermosa Inn, Paradise Valley 5
The Inn at McCormick Ranch,
    Scottsdale 6
The Lodge on the Desert,
    Tucson 9
The Wigwam, Litchfield Park 5

ARKANSAS

Crescent Hotel, Eureka Springs
    113
Dairy Hollow House, Eureka
    Springs 114
New Orleans Hotel, Eureka
    Springs 115

CALIFORNIA

Ahwahnee Hotel, Yosemite
    National Park 58
Amber House, Sacramento
    43
Apple Lane Inn, Aptos 11
The Bath Street Inn, Santa
    Barbara 54
The Beazley House, Napa 37
Bed and Breakfast Inn, San
    Francisco 47
Benbow Inn, Garberville 26
The Briggs House, Sacramento
    44
Britt House, San Diego 46
Burgundy and Bordeaux House,
    Yountville 59
Casa Madrona, Sausalito 55
Centrella Hotel, Pacific Grove
    39
City Hotel, Columbia 23
Cypress Inn, Carmel 16
Dunbar House 1880, Murphys
    37

205

1880 Union Hotel, Los Alamos 31
Eiler's Inn, Laguna Beach 30
El Cortez Hotel, San Francisco 47
The Eureka Inn, Eureka 25
Four Seasons–Clift Hotel, San Francisco 48
The Gingerbread Mansion, Ferndale 25
Glenborough Inn, Santa Barbara 54
The Gosby House Inn, Pacific Grove 40
Grape Leaf Inn, Healdsburg 27
Happy Landing Inn, Carmel 17
Hartsook Inn, Piercy 41
Holly Tree Inn, Inverness Park 28
Hotel Burgess, Reedley 42
Hotel del Coronado, Coronado 24
Hotel Léger, Mokelumne Hill 34
Hotel St. Helena, St. Helena 44
The Inn at Rancho Santa Fe, Rancho Santa Fe 41
The Jabberwock, Monterey 35
Julian Gold Rush Hotel, Julian 29
La Valencia Hotel, La Jolla 30
L'Ermitage, Beverly Hills 12
MacCallum House, Mendocino 33
The Madonna Inn, San Luis Obispo 52
Magnolia Hotel, Yountville 60
Mansion Hotel, San Francisco 49
Mendocino Hotel, Mendocino 34
Mountain Home Ranch, Calistoga 15
National Hotel, Nevada City 38
Nine Eureka Street, Sutter Creek 57
Normandy Inn, Carmel 18
The Obrero Hotel, San Francisco 50

Ojai Valley Inn and Country Club, Ojai 39
Old Monterey Inn, Monterey 36
The Old Seal Beach Inn, Seal Beach 56
Pine Inn, Carmel 19
The Raphael, San Francisco 51
Red Rooster Ranch, Los Olivos 32
St. Orres, Gualala 27
San Antonio House, Carmel 19
The Sandpiper Inn, Carmel 20
Sea View Inn, Carmel 21
Sonoma Chalet, Sonoma 56
Sonoma Mission Inn, Boyes Hot Springs 14
Sutter Creek Inn, Sutter Creek 58
Union Street Inn, San Francisco 51
The Upham Hotel, Santa Barbara 55
Vagabond House, Carmel 21
The Ventana Inn, Big Sur 13
Vintage Towers, Cloverdale 22
The Washington Square Inn, San Francisco 52
Whale Watch, Anchor Bay 10
The Wine Country Inn, St. Helena 45
Wine Way Inn, Calistoga 16


COLORADO

Briar Rose, Boulder 119
The Brown Palace, Denver 122
The General Palmer House, Durango 124
The Golden Rose Hotel, Central City 120
The Hearthstone Inn, Colorado Springs 122
Historic Redstone Inn, Redstone 129
The Home Ranch, Clark 121
Hotel Boulderado, Boulder 118
Hotel Colorado, Glenwood Springs 128

Hotel Jerome, Aspen 117
House of Yesteryears, Ouray
    128
The Neighbors, Georgetown
    127
New Sheridan Hotel, Telluride
    130
The Oxford, Denver 123
The Peck House, Empire 126
Strater Hotel, Durango 125

HAWAII

Colony Surf, Honolulu 63
Kona Village Resort,
    Kailua-Kona 64
Volcano House, Hawaii
    Volcanoes National Park
    61

IDAHO

The Idanha, Boise 75

IOWA

Die Heimat Motor Hotel,
    Homestead 156
Hotel Manning, Keosauqua 157
Mason House Inn, Bentonsport
    155

KANSAS

Rosalea's Hotel, Harper 131

LOUISIANA

The Cottage Plantation, St.
    Francisville 177
French Quarter Maisonettes,
    New Orleans 173
Lafitte Guest House, New
    Orleans 174
Lamothe House, New Orleans
    174
Maison de Ville, New Orleans
    175
Olivier House, New Orleans
    176
Propinquity, St. Francisville 178

MINNESOTA

Anderson House, Wabasha 164
Bleick House, St. Paul 161
Cascade Lodge, Grand Marais
    159
Lowell Inn, Stillwater 163
Marquette, Minneapolis 159
Palmer House Hotel, Sauk
    Centre 162
Rainy River Lodge, Baudette
    158
St. James Hotel, Red Wing 161
Schumacher's New Prague
    Hotel, New Prague 160

MISSOURI

Der Klingerbau Inn, Hermann
    165
Forest Park Hotel, St. Louis
    167
Hotel St. Genevieve, St.
    Genevieve 166

MONTANA

Chico Hot Springs, Pray 78
Izaak Walton Inn, Essex 77

NEBRASKA

Bel-Horst Inn, Belgrade 168
Fort Robinson, Crawford 169
Granada Royale Hometel,
    Omaha 170

NEVADA

The Gold Hill Hotel, Virginia
    City 65

NEW MEXICO

Broken Drum Ranch, Pecos
    133
Hotel de Vargas, Santa Fe 134
The Inn at Loretto, Santa Fe
    134
Hotel La Fonda de Taos, Taos
    136
La Fonda, Santa Fe 135

Sagebrush Inn, Taos 137
The Taos Inn, Taos 138

NORTH DAKOTA

The Rough Riders, Medora 80

OKLAHOMA

Bryan Hotel, Durant 140
Skirvin Plaza Hotel, Oklahoma
    City 141

OREGON

The Adobe Inn, Yachats 91
Ashland Hills Inn, Ashland 82
Channel House, Depoe Bay 84
Columbia Gorge Hotel, Hood
    River 86
Jacksonville Inn, Jacksonville 87
The Mallory Hotel, Portland 89
Oregon Caves Chateau, Cave
    Junction 88
Salishan Lodge, Gleneden
    Beach 84
Sunriver Lodge, Sunriver 90
Timberline Lodge, Government
    Camp 85
Tu Tu Tun Lodge, Gold Beach
    85
The Village Green, Cottage
    Grove 83
The Westin Benson, Portland
    89
Wolf Creek Tavern, Wolf
    Creek 90

SOUTH DAKOTA

State Game Lodge, Custer 93
Sylvan Lake Resort, Hill City
    94

TEXAS

Annie's Bed and Breakfast, Big
    Sandy 143
The Driskill, Austin 142
Excelsior House, Jefferson 147
La Borde House, Rio Grande
    City 150

La Mansion del Rio, San
    Antonio 150
Landmark Inn, Castroville 144
The Mansion on Turtle Creek,
    Dallas 144
The Melrose, Dallas 145
The Menger Hotel, San
    Antonio 151
New Jefferson Inn, Jefferson
    148
The Nutt House, Granbury
    146
Pride House, Jefferson 148
Prince Solms Inn, New
    Braunfels 149
St. Anthony Hotel, San
    Antonio 152
Stoneleigh Terrace, Dallas 146

UTAH

Carlton Hotel, Salt Lake City
    68
The Homestead, Midway 67
Hotel Utah, Salt Lake City 68

WASHINGTON

Beach Haven Resort, Eastsound
    97
The Captain Whidbey Inn,
    Coupeville 96
Cathlamet Hotel, Cathlamet 95
The College Inn, Seattle 103
Four Seasons Olympic Hotel,
    Seattle 104
The Inn of the White Salmon,
    White Salmon 105
James House, Port Townsend
    101
Lake Quinault Lodge, Quinault
    103
Manresa Castle, Port Townsend
    101
Outlook Inn, Eastsound 97
The Packwood Hotel,
    Packwood 100
Quimper Inn, Port Townsend
    102
Rosario Resort, Eastsound 99
Whidbey House, Langley 99

WYOMING

Hotel Wolf, Saratoga 108
Irma Hotel, Cody 106
The Parco Inn, Sinclair 108
Pine Gables Inn, Evanston
    107


CANADA

BRITISH COLUMBIA

The Four Seasons Vancouver,
    Vancouver 183
The Harrison Hotel, Harrison
    Hot Springs 181
Lake Okanagan Resort,
    Kelowna 182
Olde England Inn, Victoria
    184

Qualicum College Inn,
    Qualicum Beach 182


ONTARIO

Arowhon Pines, Algonquin
    Park 185
The Elora Mill, Elora 187
King Edward Hotel, Toronto
    189
The Millcroft Inn, Alton 186
Park Plaza Hotel, Toronto 190
The Pillar and Post Inn,
    Niagara-on-the-Lake 188
Prince of Wales Hotel,
    Niagara-on-the-Lake 189
Royal Connaught Hotel,
    Hamilton 188
The Windsor Arms Hotel,
    Toronto 190

# _Index by Inn Name

The Adobe Inn 91
Ahwahnee Hotel 58
Amber House 43
Anderson House 164
Annie's Bed and Breakfast 143
Apple Lane Inn 11
Arizona Biltmore 6
Arizona Inn 8
Arowhon Pines 185
Ashland Hills Inn 82

The Bath Street Inn 54
Beach Haven Resort 97
The Beazley House 37
Bed and Breakfast Inn 47
Bel-Horst Inn 168
Benbow Inn 26
Bleick House 161
Briar Rose 119
The Briggs House 44
Britt House 46
Broken Drum Ranch 133
The Brown Palace 122
Bryan Hotel 140
Burgundy and Bordeaux House 59

The Captain Whidbey Inn 96
Carlton Hotel 68
Casa Madrona 55
Cascade Lodge 159
Cathlamet Hotel 95
Centrella Hotel 39
Channel House 84
Chico Hot Springs 78
City Hotel 23
The Cochise Hotel 3
The College Inn 103
Colony Surf 63
Columbia Gorge Hotel 86
The Cottage Plantation 177
Crescent Hotel 113
Cypress Inn 16

Dairy Hollow House 114
Der Klingerbau Inn 165
Die Heimat Motor Hotel 156
The Driskill 142
Dunbar House 1880 37

1880 Union Hotel 31
Eiler's Inn 30
El Cortez Hotel 47

The Elora Mill 187
El Tovar Hotel 4
The Eureka Inn 25
Excelsior House 147

Forest Park Hotel 167
Fort Robinson 169
Four Seasons–Clift Hotel 48
Four Seasons Olympic Hotel
    104
The Four Seasons Vancouver
    183
French Quarter Maisonettes
    173

The General Palmer House 124
The Gingerbread Mansion 25
Glenborough Inn 54
The Golden Rose Hotel 120
The Gold Hill Hotel 65
The Gosby House Inn 40
Granada Royal Hometel 170
Grape Leaf Inn 27

Happy Landing Inn 17
The Harrison Hotel 181
Hartsook Inn 41
The Hearthstone Inn 122
Hermosa Inn 5
Historic Redstone Inn 129
Holly Tree Inn 28
The Home Ranch 121
The Homestead 67
Hotel Boulderado 118
Hotel Burgess 42
Hotel Colorado 128
Hotel del Coronado 24
Hotel de Vargas 134
Hotel Jerome 117
Hotel La Fonda de Taos 136
Hotel Léger 34
Hotel Manning 157
Hotel St. Genevieve 166
Hotel St. Helena 44
Hotel Utah 68
Hotel Wolf 108
House of Yesteryears 128

The Idanha Hotel 75
The Inn at Loretto 134

The Inn at McCormick Ranch 6
The Inn at Rancho Santa Fe 41
The Inn of the White Salmon
    105
Irma Hotel 106
Izaak Walton Inn 77

The Jabberwock 35
Jacksonville Inn 87
James House 101
Julian Gold Rush Hotel 29

King Edward Hotel 189
Kona Village Resort 64

La Borde House 150
Lafitte Guest House 174
La Fonda 135
Lake Okanagan Resort 182
Lake Quinault Lodge 103
La Mansion del Rio 150
Lamothe House 174
Landmark Inn 144
La Valencia Hotel 30
L'Ermitage 12
The Lodge on the Desert 9
Lowell Inn 163

MacCallum House 33
The Madonna Inn 52
Magnolia Hotel 60
Maison de Ville 175
Mallory Hotel 89
Manresa Castle 101
Mansion Hotel 49
The Mansion on Turtle Creek
    144
Marquette 159
Mason House 155
The Melrose 145
Mendocino Hotel 34
The Menger Hotel 151
The Millcroft Inn 186
Mountain Home Ranch 15

National Hotel 38
The Neighbors 127
New Jefferson Inn 148
New Orleans Hotel 115
New Sheridan Hotel 130

Nine Eureka Street 57
Normandy Inn 18
The Nutt House 146

The Obrero Hotel 50
Ojai Valley Inn and Country
    Club 39
Olde England Inn 184
Old Monterey Inn 36
The Old Seal Beach Inn 56
Olivier House 176
Oregon Caves Chateau 88
Outlook Inn 97
The Oxford 123

The Packwood Hotel 100
Palmer House Hotel 162
The Parco Inn 108
Park Plaza Hotel 190
The Peck House 126
The Pillar and Post Inn 188
Pine Gables Inn 107
Pine Inn 19
Pride House 148
Prince of Wales Hotel 189
Prince Solms Inn 149
Propinquity 178

Qualicum College Inn 182
Quimper Inn 102

Rainy River Lodge 158
The Raphael 51
Red Rooster Ranch 32
Rosalea's Hotel 131
Rosario Resort 99
The Rough Riders 80
Royal Connaught Hotel 188

Sagebrush Inn 137
St. Anthony Hotel 152

St. James Hotel 161
St. Orres 27
Salishan Lodge 84
San Antonio House 19
The Sandpiper Inn 20
Schumacher's New Prague
    Hotel 160
Sea View Inn 21
Skagway Inn 73
Skirvin Plaza Hotel 141
Sonoma Chalet 56
Sonoma Mission Inn 14
State Game Lodge 93
Stoneleigh Terrace 146
Strater Hotel 125
Sunriver Lodge 90
Sutter Creek Inn 58
Sylvan Lake Resort 94

The Taos Inn 138
Timberline Lodge 85
Tu Tu Tun Lodge 85

Union Street Inn 51
The Upham Hotel 55

Vagabond House 21
The Ventana Inn 13
The Village Green 83
Vintage Towers 22
Volcano House 61

The Washington Square Inn 52
The Westin Benson 89
Whale Watch 10
Whidbey House 99
The Wigwam 5
The Windsor Arms Hotel 190
The Wine Country Inn 45
Wine Way Inn 16
Wolf Creek Tavern 90